WY PLAY HOUSE

How Many Miles to Basra?
by Colin Teevan

Cast (in order of appearance)

Sophie/Jeannie Marianne Oldham

Ursula Flora Montgomery

Freddie Gareth Farr

Stewart Matthew Flynn

Dangermouse Gwilym Havard Davies

Geordie Scott Turnbull

Malek Kevork Malikyan

Tariq Emilio Doorgasingh

Director Ian Brown

Designer Jeremy Daker

Lighting Designer Guy Hoare

Sound Designer Mic Pool

Movement Director Faroque Khan

Casting Director Ginny Schiller

Assistant Director Sam Brown

Deputy Stage Manager Sarah Alford-Smith

First performance of this production:

Courtyard Theatre, West Yorkshire Playhouse, Saturday 23 September 2006

Audio Described performances: Wednesday 11 October 7.45pm & Thursday 19 October 2pm. Audio Describers: Pam Wells & Neil Scott

BSL Interpreted performance: Saturday 14 October 2.30pm.
Interpreter: Ann Marie Bracchi

Captioned performance: Wednesday 18 October 7.45pm.

There will be one interval of fifteen minutes

Production Thanks: Maryam Albasri, George Hilliar

Cast

(in order of appearance)

Marianne Oldham
Sophie/Jeannie

Trained at Bristol Old Vic Theatre School. Theatre credits include: *The Cherry Orchard* (Southwark Playhouse); *Present Laughter* (Theatre Royal, Bath/Tour); *Finally the Girl* (The Old Red Lion); *The Gentlemen from Olmedo, The Venetian Twins* (The Watermill Theatre); *We Happy Few* (Malvern Theatre); *The Tempest* (Pendley Shakespeare); *The Country Pancake* (Edinburgh Festival); *A Midsummer Night's Dream, Much Ado About Nothing* (Shakespeare Festival). Television credits include: *The World of the Impressionists*.

Flora Montgomery
Ursula

Theatre credits include: *Taming of the Shrew* (Bristol Old Vic); *Walk Hard* (Tricycle Theatre); *Dinner* (Wyndhams Theatre, West End); *A Reckoning* (Soho Theatre); *The Shape Of Things, Bash* (Gate Theatre, Dublin); *The Four Alice Bakers* (Birmingham Rep); *Miss Julie* (Best Actress – Irish Times Theatre Award), *Drive On* (Lyric Theatre, Belfast); *Hamlet* (Norwich Playhouse); *Gaslight* (English National Tour); *Loco Country Lonesome* (Irish National Tour/Olympia Theatre Dublin). Television credits include: *Midsomer Murders, Inspector Murdoch Mysteries, Under The Dragon's Lair, Pulling Moves, Hans Christian Anderson, Monarch of the Glen, Body Story, Urban Gothic , Metropolis, Poirot, An Unsuitable Job for a Woman, A Certain Justice, Under The Sun, Wuthering Heights, Mosley, The Perfect Blue, Bugs, The Governor, The Bill, Ultimate Force*. Film credits include: *Basic Instinct 2, After, Rabbit Fever, Speed Dating, Man to Man, Benedict Arnold, Goldfish Memory* (Best Actress – Monte Carlo Film Festival & Shooting Star - Berlin Film Festival), *Discovery of Heaven, When Brendan met Trudy* (Best Actress – Las Palmas Film Festival). Flora has performed numerous plays and stories for Radio 4 and has just presented a documentary for the BBC.

Gareth Farr
Freddie

Trained at Webster Douglas Academy. Theatre credits include: *The Long, The Short & The Tall* (Sheffield Crucible); *Harvest* (Royal Court); *Romeo and Juliet* (Derby Playhouse); *Brassed Off* (York Theatre Royal); *Hobsons Choice* (Young Vic/ UK Tour); *Parting Shots* (Stephen Joseph Theatre, Scarborough); *The Taming of the Shrew, Fen, Sharp Relief* (Salisbury Playhouse); *A Midsummer Night's Dream* (RSC). Television credits include: *A Life Beyond, The Box, The Bill, Turkish Delight, Jonathan Creek, Heartbeat*.

Matthew Flynn
Stewart

Theatre credits include: *A Winter's Tale* (Brooklyn Academy, New York/ International Tour); *Romeo and Juliet* (Derby Playhouse); *The Mayor of Zalamea* (Liverpool Everyman); *A Midsummer Night's Dream* (National Tour/West End); *A View from the Bridge* (National Tour); *Rose Rage* (National Tour/Theatre Royal Haymarket); *The Prince of Homburg* (RSC/Lyric Hammersmith); *Meat* (Plymouth Theatre Royal); *Hamlet* (Bristol Old Vic); *Twelfth Night, The Comedy Of Errors, Henry V, Othello* (Propeller Theatre/ National & International Tour); *Julius*

Caesar, Romeo and Juliet (RSC); *Julius Caesar* (Royal Exchange Manchester); *Ideal Husband* (West End/Tour); *Egon Schiele* (Jay McDee Co.); *Iago* (Steam Factory). Television credits include: *Coronation Street, After Thomas, The Quatermass Experiment, Midsummer Murders, Foyles War, Trial And Retribution, Hello, Doctors.* Film credits include: *Sahara, Tell Me No Lies, The Final Passage*.

Gwilym Havard Davies
Dangermouse

Trained at the University of Durham and the Oxford School of Drama. Theatre credits include: *The Boy Who Fell into a Book* (English Touring Theatre); *Precious Bane* (Pentabus). Theatre credits whilst training include: *After the Dance, Pillars of the Community*. Television credits include: *Torchwood, Life Begins*. Film credits include: *The Run*.

Scott Turnbull
Geordie

Trained at Liverpool Institute of Performing Arts. *How Many Miles to Basra?* marks Scott's professional theatre debut. Theatre credits whilst at LIPA include: *Oh What a Lovely War, Romeo and Juliet, Can't Pay? Won't Pay!, Twelfth Night*. Television credits include: *Byker Grove* (regular character).

Kevork Malikyan
Malek

Theatre credits include: *Stuff Happens, The Ends of the Earth* (National Theatre); *Homebody Kabul* (Young Vic/Cheek by Jowl); *Barefoot in the Park* (Theatre Royal, Northampton); *Pera Palas* (National Theatre Studio/Gate Theatre); *Servant of Two Masters, Measure for Measure, Bartholomew Fair, Twelfth Night* (RSC); *Waiting for Godot* (Lyric, Hammersmith/ The Drum, Plymouth). Television credits include: *Spooks, Casualty, Discovering Egypt, Dr Who, The Saint, The Avengers, Minder, The Professionals, Mind Your Language* (TV series), *House of Cards, Into the Blue* (all UK). *Remington Steel, Scarecrow and Mrs King, MacGyver, The Three Musketeers, The Corsican Brothers, In the Beginning, The Bible, Young Indie Chronicles* (all USA). Film credits include: *Flight of the Phoenix, The Commissioner, Double Vision, Indiana Jones and the Last Crusade, Pascalis Island, Ishtar, Half Moon Street, Sphinx, Midnight Express, The Thief of Baghdad, Scorpio, The Man Who Haunted Himself*.

Emilio Doorgasingh
Tariq

Theatre credits include: *Angels Among the Trees* (Nottingham Playhouse); *Change of Heart* (New End Theatre); *A Midsummer Night's Dream* (Comedy Theatre/ International Tour); *Rose Rage* (Haymarket Theatre/International Tour); *The Ramayana* (National Theatre); *Dial M for Murder* (English Theatre Of Frankfurt); *Twelfth Night* (Watermill Theatre, Newbury); *The Comedy of Errors* (Watermill Theatre/ World Tour); *The Middle Class Tendency* (Wimbledon Theatre); *Henry V* (Watermill Theatre/German Tour); *The Magic Toyshop* (One From The Heart Theatre Co); *Saying Yes* (The Gate); *Dreams of Clytemnestra* (BAC); *Dangers of Common Sense* (Lewisham Theatre); *Cymbeline* (Etcetera Theatre); *A Midsummer Night's Dream* (The Production Village). Television credits include: *Untitled History Project, Hannibal, Miss Marple, Rebus, The Bill, Neanderthal, In My Dreams, King David, Anton and Minty, Uncle Jack* and *Cleopatra's Mummy*. Film credits include: *Rendition, Kingdom of Heaven, Guru in Seven*.

Creatives

Colin Teevan *Writer*

Colin Teevan was born in Dublin. His stage plays include: *The Bee*, co-written with Hideki Noda (Soho Theatre); *Missing Persons: Four Tragedies and Roy Keane* (Assembly Rooms, Edinburgh/Trafalgar Studios) *Cock of the North* – published as *Alcmaeon in Corinth* (Newcastle Live!); *Monkey!* (The Young Vic/Dundee Rep); *The Walls* (National Theatre); *Svejk*, from the novel by Jaroslav Hasek (Gate London/The Duke, New York); *Vinegar and Brown Paper* (Abbey, Dublin); *The Big Sea* (Galloglass Ireland/Riverside Studios). Stage translations include: from Ancient Greek: *Iph...* after Euripides' *Iphigenia in Aulis* (Lyric Belfast); *Bacchai* by Euripides (National Theatre/Epidaurus, Greece); *Marathon* by Edoardo Erba (Gate London); *Cuckoos* by Giuseppe Manfridi (Gate London/Barbican). Radio plays include: *Iph...*, *Tricycles*, *The RoyKeaneiad Parts 1 and 2*, *Medea: The Last Word* and *How Many Miles to Basra?*, all BBC Radio 3. Colin was the production dramaturg and associate director on Peter Hall's *Tantalus* (RSC/Denver Center for Performing Arts). He was writer-in-residence at Queen's University, Belfast; Screen East Writing Fellow at UEA and North Eastern Literary Fellow based at the Universities of Newcastle and Durham. He is currently lecturer in dramatic writing at the University of Newcastle. All his work is published by Oberon Books. Forthcoming projects include: *The Seven Pomegranate Seeds* with Clare Higgins (Onassis Foundation) and adaptations of *The Odyssey* (Northern Stage) and *Don Quixote* (West Yorkshire Playhouse).

Ian Brown *Director*

Ian was appointed Artistic Director and Chief Executive of the West Yorkshire Playhouse in 2003, where he has directed *Foxes*, *Alice in Wonderland*, *Twelfth Night*, *The Lion, the Witch and the Wardrobe* (nominated for a TMA Award), *Electricity*, *The Wind in the Willows*, *A Small Family Business*, *Pretending to be Me* with Tom Courtenay, *Hamlet* with Christopher Eccleston, *The Lady in the Van*, *Hijra*, *Eden End*, *Stepping Out*, *Broken Glass*, *The Comedy of Errors*, *Proposals*, *You'll Have Had Your Hole* by Irvine Welsh and *Of Mice and Men*. Ian was also Associate Artistic Director of the Playhouse for two years from 2001 to 2003. Other theatre credits include: *Equus* (Beer Sheva Theatre, Israel); *Goodnight Children Everywhere*, which won the Olivier Award for Best New Play, *Victoria* by David Greig (RSC); *Five Kinds of Silence* (Out of the Blue Productions); *Strangers on a Train* (Colchester/Guildford/Richmond); *Babycakes* (Drill Hall); *Fool for Love* (Donmar Warehouse); *Widows* by Ariel Dorfman (Traverse Theatre, Edinburgh); *Steaming* (Piccadilly Theatre); *Nabokov's Gloves* (Hampstead Theatre); *Killing Rasputin* (Bridewell Theatre); the original production of *Trainspotting* (Citizen's Theatre/The Bush Theatre). From 1988 to 1999 Ian was Artistic Director and Chief Executive of the Traverse Theatre, Edinburgh. Productions included: *Reader*, *The Collection*, *Unidentified Human Remains and the True Nature of Love*, *Poor Super Man* (Evening Standard Award), *Ines de Castro*, *Light in the Village*, *Moscow Stations* with Tom Courtenay (Evening Standard Award, Best Actor), *Hanging the President* (Scotsman Fringe First), *The Bench, Hardie and Baird* by David Kelman, *Bondagers* by Sue Glover (which won the Scotland on Sunday Award and transferred to the Donmar Warehouse and World Stage Festival, Toronto), *Shining Souls*. In 1999 Ian was awarded a Scotsman Fringe First and a Herald Angel Award for his work at the Traverse. Ian was also Artistic Director of TAG Theatre Company, Citizen's Theatre for five years, where productions included: *Othello*, *A Midsummer Night's Dream*, *As You Like It*, *Romeo and Juliet*, *Hard Times*, *Can't Pay? Won't Pay!*, *Great Expectations* (Spirit of Mayfest Award).

Before directing, Ian trained as a teacher and taught in a London comprehensive School. He became a Community Arts worker at the Cockpit Theatre in London and ran the Cockpit Youth Theatre. In 1982 he got his first professional job in theatre at the Theatre Royal Stratford East where he became Associate Director.

Jeremy Daker *Designer*

Jeremy graduated from the Motley Theatre Design Course. Design credits include: *Of Mice & Men* (Mercury Theatre, Colchester); *Turned on Tap* (Royal Festival Hall); *Mayhem* (Royal Exchange, Manchester); *Ministry of Pleasure* (Latchmere Theatre); *Alabaster City, Resident Alien* (Tristan Bates Theatre); *Lear* (Royal National Theatre Studio); *Comedy of Vanity* (Union Theatre/Edinburgh Festival). Assistant design credits include: *Daddy Cool* (Shaftesbury Theatre); *The Gondoliers* (ENO); *5/11*, Minerva Theatre Seasons 2004 & 2005, *Three Women and A Piano Tuner, Seven Doors, The Seagull, Holes in the Skin* (Chichester Festival Theatre); *Three Women and a Piano Tuner* (Hampstead Theatre); *The Bitter Tears of Petra Von Cant* (English National Opera); *Asscanio in Alba, Merry Wives* (Buxton Opera House); *Cav & Pag* (Dallas Opera House); *Capriccio* (Lincoln Centre, New York); *Rheingold* and *Gotterdammerung* as part of the *Ring* Cycle (Brazil); *Girl in a Goldfish Bowl* (Sheffield Crucible Theatre); Five New plays at the 2004 Young Playwright's Festival (Royal Court Theatre); *Macbeth* (Dundee Rep); *The Beat* (Arcola Theatre); *Twilight of the Gods* (English National Opera); *Daphne* (Lincoln Centre, New York); *L'Elsir d'Amore* (Tiroler Landestheatre); *Singer* (Tricycle Theatre); *When Harry Met Sally* (Theatre Royal, Haymarket); *Broken Fiction* (Linbury Studio, Royal Opera House); *Sergeant Musgraves Dance* (UK Tour); *Hobson's Choice* (Young Vic Theatre); *Richard III* (RSC). Jeremy was also a finalist of the Linbury Biennial Prize 2003.

Guy Hoare *Lighting Designer*

Theatre credits include: *Season's Greetings* (Liverpool Playhouse); *Of Mice and Men* (Mecury Theatre, Colchester); *A Streetcar Named Desire* (Clwyd Theatr Cymru); *The Little Fir Tree, Fen, Far Away, Macbeth* (Sheffield Theatres); *Zero Degrees and Drifting…, Could It Be Magic?* (Unlimited Theatre); *Crossings* (Sgript Cymru); *Frankie & Johnny in the Clair De Lune* (Sound Theatre); *Old Times, Love in the Title, Frozen, The Caretaker, Closer, Entertaining Mr Sloane, Molly Sweeney, The Killing of Sister George, Someone Who'll Watch Over Me, Look Back in Anger, The Game of Love and Chance, My Mother Said I Never Should, Oleanna* (UK tours for London Classic Theatre); *The Ballad of Johnny 5 Star* (Library Theatre, Manchester); *Observe the Sons of Ulster Marching Towards the Somme* (Pleasance Theatre, London); *Live Bed Show, Walking Backwards to Brighton* (Royal Theatre, Northampton); *Story of an African Farm* (Young Vic Studio); *666, The Alchemist, Play, The Ritual* (Riverside Studios); *Presto* (Royal Exchange Studio, Manchester); *Landscape of the Body, Marisol* (Southwark Playhouse); *Soho, Marat/Sade* (Arcola Theatre). Opera, Musicals and Concert credits include: *Tracy Beaker Gets Real* (Nottingham Playhouse/UK Tour); *Assassins* (Sheffield Theatres); *Das Rheingold, Die Walküre, Siegfried, Götterdämmerung, The Magic Flute, Tosca, Hansel & Gretel* (Longborough Festival Opera); *Cinderella* (ROH Education); *Names of the Dead, Venus & Adonis, Lost in the Stars, Treemonisha, The Cradle Will Rock* (BAC); *Tosca, Cosi Fan Tutte* (Opera UK); *The Music of Steve Reich, A Tribute to Xenakis* (Purcell Room). Dance credits include: Resident Designer for Henri Oguike Dance Company since 2000, *Tiger Dancing, Expression Lines, Second Signal, White Space, Frames Per Second Parts 1 & 2, Finale, Dido & Aeneas, Frontline, In Broken Tendrils, Melancholy Thoughts, Shot Flow, A Moment of Give* (UK/Europe/Middle East Tours); *Sea of Bones, Bad History, Green Apples, Dive*

(Mark Bruce Company); *Flicker* (Shobana Jeyasingh Dance Company); *Odyssey* (Krische/Wright Company); *Goodbye Venus, Viking Shoppers* (Igloo); *Show, Spirit Level, Bye, Flap, Small Hours, Orange Gina, Sleep Talking, Lonely Hearts/ Suspicious Minds* (The Snag Project).

Mic Pool *Sound Designer*

In a twenty-nine year career in theatre sound, Mic has been resident at the Lyric Theatre Hammersmith, the Royal Court Theatre, Tyne Theatre Company and toured internationally with Ballet Rambert. He has designed the sound for over 300 productions including more than 180 for the West Yorkshire Playhouse where he is currently Director of Creative Technology. He received a TMA award in 1992 for Best Designer (Sound) for *Life Is A Dream* and was nominated for both the Lucille Lortel and the Drama Desk Award for Outstanding Sound Design 2001 for the New York production of *The Unexpected Man*. Recent theatre credits include: *The Postman Always Rings Twice* (Playhouse Theatre); *Ying Tong* (New Ambassadors Theatre); *The Solid Gold Cadillac* (Garrick Theatre); *Brand* (RSC and West End); *Pretending To Be Me* (West Yorkshire Playhouse/West End); *Art* (West End/Broadway/worldwide); *Shockheaded Peter* (Cultural Industry world tour/West End); *The Unexpected Man* (RSC/West End/Broadway/Los Angeles); *Another Country* (Arts Theatre); *Beauty and the Beast, A Midsummer Night's Dream, The Seagull, Victoria, Romeo and Juliet, Twelfth Night, The Roundhouse Season of Late Shakespeare Plays* (RSC); *Three Thousand Troubled Threads* (Stellar Quines, Edinburgh International Festival); *Blues in the Night, A Doll's House, David Copperfield, The 39 Steps, Twelfth Night, My Mother Said I Never Should, Alice in Wonderland, Dead Funny, Bad Girls – The Musical* (West Yorkshire Playhouse); *Homage to Catalonia* (West Yorkshire Playhouse/ Northern Stage/Teatre Romea). Video designs for theatre includes: *Der Ring des Nibelungen* (Royal Opera House, Covent Garden); *Three Thousand Troubled Threads* (Stellar Quines, Edinburgh International Festival); *The Solid Gold Cadillac* (West End); *Dracula* (The Touring Consortium); *The Lion, The Witch and the Wardrobe, The Wizard of Oz, Johnson Over Jordan, Crap Dad, Scuffer* (West Yorkshire Playhouse); *Dangerous Corner* (West Yorkshire Playhouse/West End); *Singin' In The Rain* (West Yorkshire Playhouse/Royal National Theatre/national tour); *The Turk In Italy* (ENO); *The Ring Cycle* (New National Theatre Tokyo); *Il Tabarro, Chorus!* (WNO); *Of Mice and Men* (Mind the Gap). Television includes the sound design for *How Wide is Your Sky* (Real Life Productions for Channel Four); *Lesley Garrett and Friends At The Movies* (BBC).

Faroque Khan
Movement Director

Trained: Strathclyde University (B.A. in Community Arts), Pantheatre- France, Krauses International Martial Arts Academy. Director credits include: *Tagged* (Red Ladder Theatre Company), *Jihad: Inner Struggle* (Theatre Insaan), Associate Director on *The Lion, the Witch and the Wardrobe* (West Yorkshire Playhouse). Movement Director credits include: *The Lion, the Witch and the Wardrobe, Wind in the Willows, Medea, Hamlet, Hijra* (West Yorkshire Playhouse); *A Midsummer Night's Dream, Macbeth* (Derby Playhouse); *Bloodtide, Unsuitable Girls, Rumblefish, Lord of the Flies* (Pilot Theatre Company); *Masala Nights, Soulskin* (Red Ladder Theatre Company). Acting credits include: *Jihad: Inner Struggle* (Theatre Insaan); *The Chimp That Spoke* (David Glass Ensemble); *OneTwo* (Suspect Culture); *Unsuitable Girls, Lord of the Flies* (Pilot Theatre Company); *Faustuslite* (Rose Theatre Co); *Pandora's Box* (Panthetare UK); *Twelfth Night* (National Theatre Education); *Caucasian Chalk Circle* (Complicite). Television credits include: *Horizon Special, Walking with Cavemen, Inspector Rebus, Ruth Rendell Mysteries,*

Kismet Road. Film credits include: *Umnachtung*.

Ginny Schiller
Casting Director

Recent theatre credits include: *The Canterbury Tales* (tour/West End) and the Complete Works Festival for the RSC; *The Old Country, Hamlet* (both tours and West End transfers), *Mother Courage and Her Children, Rosencrantz and Guildenstern are Dead* and *Twelfth Night* for ETT; three years as Casting Director for Soho Theatre, where credits include *Blue Eyes & Heels, Shoreditch Madonna, A Reckoning* and *Colder than Here*. Also *All My Sons* (Liverpool Playhouse); *Present Laughter* (Theatr Clwyd); *The Taming of the Shrew* (Bristol Old Vic); *The Importance of Being Earnest* (Oxford Playhouse); *A Passage to India* (Shared Experience); *When the World was Green* (Young Vic); *Macbeth* (Albery); three seasons for Chichester Festival Theatre and five years with the RSC. Television and film credits include: *Notes on a Scandal, George Orwell – A Life in Pictures* (Emmy Award Winner), *The Bill, The Falklands Play*. Radio credits include: *The Pickwick Papers, Tender is the Night, The Bride's Chamber*.

Sam Brown
Assistant Director

Sam is currently assistant director in residence at the Playhouse and is studying for the Arts Council MFA in Theatre Directing at Birkbeck College, London. Before coming to Leeds he directed *Bussmann's Holiday* (59 East 59th St. Theatre, New York and Assembly Rooms, Edinburgh). He has worked at the Young Vic with Matthew Dunster and at Drama Centre London with Annie Tyson and he assisted Erica Whyman (Northern Stage) on *The Importance of Being Earnest* (Oxford Playhouse). Directing credits include: *Elegies for Angels, Punks & Raging Queens* (Oxford Playhouse); *Julius Caesar* for Thelma Holt (tour of Japan); *Mongoose* (Burton Taylor); *Picasso at*

the Lapin Agile (Old Fire Station); *The Night Before Christmas, Pre Paradise Sorry Now* and *Falsettos* - UK premiere (O'Reilly Theatre). From 2001 to 2003 he was design consultant and theatre director of the O'Reilly Theatre in Oxford. Future projects include: *The Duchess of Malfi* (assisting Philip Franks); Leeds City Council's Light Night programme, Northern Exposure.

West Yorkshire Playhouse

Since opening in 1990, West Yorkshire Playhouse has established a reputation both nationally and internationally as one of Britain's most exciting and active producing theatres, winning awards for everything from its productions to its customer service. The Playhouse provides both a thriving focal point for the communities of West Yorkshire and theatre of the highest standard for audiences throughout the region and beyond.

West Yorkshire Playhouse works regularly with other major regional producing theatres including Birmingham Rep in 2004 to create *The Madness of George III* and *A View from the Bridge* and again in 2006 for *Alice in Wonderland, To Kill A Mockingbird* and the forthcoming production of *The Wizard of Oz*. Also, in 2006, the Playhouse joined forces with Liverpool Theatres on a co-production of *Hedda Gabler* and with Big Broad and Shed Productions to create *Bad Girls – The Musical*.

Other collaborations have included a new production and subsequent tour of *Wars of the Roses* with Northern Broadsides; *Homage to Catalonia* with Teatre Romea and Northern Stage and *The Bacchae*, a co-production with Kneehigh Theatre which also toured nationally. Recent successful London transfers include *Ying Tong* to the New Ambassadors in association with Michael Codron, and *The Postman Always Rings Twice*, which transferred to the Playhouse Theatre with Ambassador Theatre Group, as well as *Bat Boy The Musical* and *Pretending to Be Me* starring Tom Courtenay.

Leeds Theatre Trust Ltd.

Paint Shop

Virginia Whiteley *Head Scenic Artist*

Performance Staff

Andy Charlesworth and Jon Murray *Firemen*

Andrew Ashdown, Daisy Babbington, Isobel Bainton, Kathryn Beale, Rachel Blackeby, Alexandra Bradshaw, Andrew Bramma, Jennifer Bramma, Dean Burke, Megan Case, Lindsey Chapman, Chandy Chima, Megan Christie, Joe Churchill, Jez Coram, Sarah Cullen, Tony Duggan, Amy Fawdington, Corinne Furness, Rory Girvan, Andrew Gilpin, Emma Goodway, Deb Hargrave, Becky Harding, Fiona Heseltine, Joanna Hutt, Rachel Kendall, Alexandra Lavelle, Robert Long, Victoria Long, Allan Mawson, Rionach McDaid-Wren, Gordon McNaughton, Michelle Moseley, Lindsay Murray, Hayley Mort, Jo Murray, Katie Powers, Sarah Roughley, Pam Sandhu, Tim Sharry, Jayne Thompson, Daneill Whyles, and Rebekah Wilkes *Attendants**

Press

Rachel Coles *Head of Press*

Leonie Osborne *Acting Head of Press*

Katie Turner *Assistant Press Officer*

Michael Eppy *Press Assistant*

Production Electricians

Matt Young *Chief Electrician*

David Bennion-Pedley *Deputy Chief Electrician*

Paul Halgarth, Chris Alexander and Elizabeth Moran *Electricians*

Andrew Bolton *Freelance Electrician*

Production Management

Suzi Cubbage *Production Manager*

Eddie de Pledge *Production Manager*

Dickon Harold *Head of Technical Design*

Christine Alcock *Production Administrator*

Props Department

Chris Cully *Head of Props*

Sarah Barry Deputy *Head of Props*

Susie Cockram and Scott Thompson *Prop Makers*

Restaurant and Bar

Michael Montgomery *Head Chef*

Louise Poulter *Chef de Partie*

Kirsty Crerar and Linda Monaghan *Commis Chefs*

Robert Cawood, Lee Moran and Robert Wright *Kitchen Porters*

Diane Kendall and Pauline Wilkes-Ruan *Restaurant Supervisors*

Lee Dennell, Jade Gough, Caron Hawley, Kath Langton* and Esther Lewis *Restaurant Assistants*

Alice Baxter, Rosanna Gordon, Cheryl Lee, Cati MacKenzie, Rachel Marriner, Sinead Rodgers, Hayley Smith, Justine Tong, William White and Jenny Yan *Restaurant Assistants**

Chris Alston *Bar Manager*

Terrence Whitlam *Bar Supervisor*

Elizabeth Carter, Kit Beaumont, Gabriel Clark, Joseph Crithcley, Paul Douglas, Adam Featherstone, Dean Firth, Rachel Frederick, Giles Green, Tracey Hodgetts, Abbie Johnson, Zoë Kirk, Jodie Marshall, Victoria Monk, Ben Richardson, Robert Stevenson, Lucy Wright and Karlene Wray *Bar Assistants**

Gemma Schoffield *Coffee Shop Assistant*

Scenic Construction

Andrew Dye *Head of Construction*

Gavin Bryan Deputy *Head of Construction*

Julian Hibbert and Sally Langford Carpenters and *Metal Workers*

Jimmy Ragg *Carpenter*

Andrew Wood and Graham Pedley *Freelance Carpenter*

Security

Denis Bray *Security Manager*

Glenn Slowther *Security Officer*

Mayfair *Security*

Sound Department

Andrew Meadows *Head of Sound*

Martin Pickersgill *Deputy Head of Sound*

Mathew Angove *Assistant Sound Technician*

Technical Stage Management

Martin S Ross *Technical Stage Manager*

Michael Cassidy *Deputy Technical Stage Manager*

Nidge Solly *Stage Technician*

David Berrell, Matt Hooban, Marc Walton and Matt de Pledge *Stage Crew*

Theatre Operations

Jeni Chillingsworth *House Manager*

Jonathan Dean, Tony Duggan, Sheila Howarth and Stuart Simpson *Duty Managers*

Wardrobe Department

Stephen Snell *Head of Wardrobe*

Victoria Marzetti *Deputy Head of Wardrobe*

Julie Ashworth *Head Cutter*

Nicole Martin *Cutter*

Alison Barrett *Costume Prop Maker/Dyer*

Victoria Harrison and Catherine Lowe *Wardrobe Assistants*

Gabriel Hamilton *Wig and Make-up Supervisor*

Catherine Newton *Wardrobe Maintenance/ Head Dresser*

Anne Marie Hewitt *Costume Hire Manager*

* *Denotes part-time*

WEST YORKSHIRE PLAYHOUSE
CORPORATE SUPPORTERS

Sponsors of the Spark Project

PROVIDENT
FINANCIAL

Production Sponsors

 Hedda Gabler

Directors' Club

Executive Members

 EVANS property group

leeds metropolitan university

 Carlsberg

Associate Members

YORKSHIRE POST

 ITV YORKSHIRE

Director Members

Halifax plc   Provident Financial   Matthew Clark   InBev UK Ltd

West Yorkshire Playhouse gratefully acknowledges support from

BBC northern exposure

M
Millennium Commission
LOTTERY FUNDED

CHARITABLE TRUSTS

Audrey and Stanley Burton 1960 Trust   Harewood Charitable Settlement
Kenneth Hargreaves Charitable Trust   The Frances Muers Trust
Clothworkers' Foundation   The Charles Brotherton Trust
The Ragdoll Foundation   Harold Hyam Wingate Foundation

If you would like to learn how your organisation can become involved with the success of the West Yorkshire Playhouse please contact the Development Department on 0113 213 7275.

HOW MANY MILES TO BASRA?

First published in 2006 by Oberon Books Ltd.
521 Caledonian Road, London N7 9RH
Tel: 020 7607 3637 / Fax: 020 7607 3629
e-mail: info@oberonbooks.com
www.oberonbooks.com

A catalogue record for this book is available from the British Library.

ISBN: 1 84002 690 1

Cover image: Corbis

Printed in Great Britain by Antony Rowe Ltd, Chippenham.

Characters

SOPHIE

URSULA

FREDDIE

STEWART

DANGERMOUSE

GEORDIE

SAYED

MALEK

BANDIT

TARIQ

JEANNIE

How Many Miles to Basra? was first written as a radio play and broadcast on 11 July 2004 on BBC Radio 3, produced by Toby Swift.

The author wishes to express his grateful thanks to the following for their help in developing this script: Paul Adams, Maryam Albasri, Lewis Alsamari, Hakim Sammy Belkhiri, Ian Brown, Sam Brown, Jonathan Charles, Alex Chisholm, Madeline Dewhurst, George Hilliar, Charlie Hopkinson, Toby Swift, Tim Whewell, and all the actors who have taken part in the radio broadcast, studio workshops and stage production of *How Many Miles to Basra?*

Notes

> A speech indented and presented in this font is interview material, and is not part of the narrative of the scene in which it may appear. It may be performed direct to audience, through microphone or as voice-over.

Translations appear in square brackets after the lines to which they refer.

The following text went to press during rehearsals and may differ slightly from the play as performed.

Act One

1: THE EDITOR'S OFFICE

SOPHIE sits at a table with a stack of minidiscs and a minidisc player. She listens to recordings on headphones, skipping through them making notes. She finishes one disc and moves onto the next. Enter URSULA. SOPHIE does not hear. She finishes another, returns it to its case and is about to load a third when she becomes aware of URSULA. She knocks a pile of discs to the floor.

SOPHIE: Shit!

SOPHIE scrabbles on the floor to retrieve discs.

URSULA: I'm ever so…

URSULA kneels down.

Please, let me –

SOPHIE: No, please, they were in order. I was putting them in order. Thanks anyway.

URSULA: I didn't mean to sneak up on you.

SOPHIE: No, I'm sorry, world of my own. (*Gesturing to headphones.*) The cans.

They both stand.

URSULA: Actually I was looking for Tariq. He is still editor?

SOPHIE: Yes. Yes, he's just in a meeting. Can I help? I'm his assistant, Sophie. Intern, actually.

URSULA: I had an appointment. I'm –

SOPHIE: Ursula!

URSULA: Yes.

SOPHIE: Ursula Gunn, of course! I'm sorry. I should have…
You're nothing like –

URSULA: How I look on radio?

SOPHIE: Yes. I mean no. I'm sorry.

URSULA: There's one more?

SOPHIE: Excuse me?

URSULA: Disc. On the floor.

URSULA picks it up. She is about to hand it to SOPHIE when something catches her eye. SOPHIE moves to take it, but URSULA withdraws it.

SOPHIE: I really am sorry. Tariq told me you were coming. I was just distracted with the discs. Your recordings, in fact.

URSULA: Yes.

SOPHIE: Tariq asked me to see you. Not instead of him, but while you were waiting. I was expecting them to buzz up. Would you like a coffee or tea? There's a new coffee truck by the lift. It does everything: cappucino, latte…

URSULA: No, thanks.

Pause.

SOPHIE: He's with the lawyers. And Head of Radio News. You weren't in a rush anywhere were you?

URSULA: I've an appointment later. Colchester. No.

SOPHIE: That's good. (*Pause.*) It's about the 'sexing up'.

URSULA: What is?

SOPHIE: His meeting. You haven't heard the news?

URSULA: Been a bit out of circulation.

SOPHIE: Of course. It must have been –

URSULA: So what's this news?

SOPHIE: The Government lied to us.

URSULA: That's news?

SOPHIE: About Iraq.

URSULA: Tariq told me Iraq was old news four weeks ago.

SOPHIE: A source in the Intelligence Service told Andrew Gilligan that the Government asked Intelligence to sex up the dossier on Saddam's weapon capabilities. And the Government then published the dossier knowing it to contain false claims. And Andy went on air with it earlier in the week, and since then the place has gone mad. The Prime Minister's office has been piling the pressure on the Head of News, and they've been putting the pressure on the heads of departments, and so we're having to go through everything with a fine-tooth comb. Even Tariq's under pressure and he'd nothing to do with it. That's why he asked me to log your recordings. I wasn't really listening to them, just dates and places and interviewees.

URSULA: But I have a record of them.

URSULA hands SOPHIE the disc.

SOPHIE: He wanted an official record.

URSULA: Has he actually listened to them yet?

SOPHIE: Oh, I'm sure he has.

Pause.

I'm a big fan of yours. I mean I admire your work enormously.

URSULA: Thank you.

SOPHIE: Tariq is too.

URSULA: He said?

SOPHIE: He said your work's different. (*Beat.*) What was it like out in Iraq?

URSULA: Different. (*Beat.*) Show me this log of yours.

SOPHIE: It's not finished –

URSULA takes the clipboard from SOPHIE anyway.

But I haven't finished it.

URSULA: What kind of order's this?

SOPHIE: Chronological. From April 13th –

URSULA: But that's not the right order. You can't tell the story like that. That's not how it happened.

URSULA unplugs headphones and connects speakers and presses play.

Start with this one.

URSULA sits and takes out a tobacco tin.

SOPHIE: I'm afraid you can't smoke –

URSULA: I don't smoke.

FREDDIE is revealed.

> FREDDIE: Yeah, I'd say morale was low. I mean, look at it: this country. What the fuck are we doing here? It's not like they're grateful or anything. It's not like the people at home even want us here in the first place. So who the fuck are we fighting this for?

FREDDIE rolls a cigarette while he listens to a question.

SOPHIE: Which one's this?

URSULA: Freddie.

> FREDDIE: Well, quite apart from the blindingly
> obvious like no body armour and noddy suits,
> there weren't even enough desert boots. We're
> fighting a war in the desert with no desert boots.
> I had to buy my fucking own. I would have liked
> to have seen some action, that's what it's all
> about, isn't it? But with the kit they've sent us out
> here with, I'm happy that we'll soon be headed
> home –

URSULA presses stop. FREDDIE remains where he is and lights the cigarette.

URSULA: No. No, I should start with the VCP.

SOPHIE: VCP?

URSULA: Vehicle checkpoint.

SOPHIE: That's where the Unit helped out the Bedouin?

URSULA: Helped out? Is that what the MoD said?

SOPHIE: That's what they said on the news.

URSULA: You shouldn't believe everything you hear. It was
April 15th, on the Jalibah road. I was up on an escarpment,
a wadi bank, with Geordie. Stewart and Freddie and
Dangermouse were down by the road...

2: THE VEHICLE CHECKPOINT

A vehicle checkpoint on the Jalibah Road, Southern Iraq, the afternoon of April 15th, 2003. STEWART and DANGERMOUSE are now in position with FREDDIE. They wait, tense and bored. FREDDIE continues to smoke. Silence.

STEWART: Time, Dangermouse.

DANGERMOUSE: 1530, boss.

FREDDIE: Four hours. Four fucking hours and not even a goat.

DANGERMOUSE: Call this an MSR, eh Fred?

FREDDIE: Main supply route between the arsehole and nowhere. What the fuck are we doing here?

DANGERMOUSE: Fucked if I know.

STEWART: We are operating a vehicle checkpoint, boys.

FREDDIE: I mean this country, this fucking country, what are we doing here?

STEWART: Let's leave the morality to the politicians to worry about. More to the point, what's Geordie doing up there?

DANGERMOUSE: Up where?

STEWART: On the escarp with Ursula.

DANGERMOUSE: Looks like he's holding her sat-dish, boss.

STEWART: I can see that, Danger, but he's meant to be watching our backs.

FREDDIE: (*Impersonating URSULA.*) This is Ursula Gunn, it is April 15th 2003 and I am standing at a crucial vehicle checkpoint on the Jalibah road with Private Dangermouse of the Third Royals. Private Dangermouse, could you tell me how it feels?

DANGERMOUSE: How what feels, Freddie?

FREDDIE: (*Impersonating URSULA.*) Being here, Private Dangermouse, in Iraq, one week after the fall of Saddam's statue, what does it feel like, Private Dangermouse, the white heat of war?

DANGERMOUSE: Well, it's hot, out here, Fred, I mean Ursula. I mean it's a desert, isn't it?

FREDDIE: She asked me to do an interview for her –

DANGERMOUSE: I did one for her and all.

FREDDIE: About morale. About morale being low.

STEWART: What did you say?

FREDDIE: I told her of course it's low. I mean half the country
don't want us here. And it's not like the natives are
overjoyed to see us either. And as for the kit they sent us
out with –

STEWART: Jesus Freddie!

FREDDIE: No, I didn't, I told her to fuck off. I don't have to
give that nosey bitch any interviews. Not in my contract.

DANGERMOUSE: What about you, boss? You talk to her?

STEWART: No. No more than I had to. Whatever you say, say
nothing.

FREDDIE: At least we won't have to put up with her much
longer. Hear all the journalists are being withdrawn.

STEWART: Iraq's old news already.

FREDDIE: Knew it was going to be a bad war when they gave
us a woman journalist. And a radio journalist at that!

STEWART: Still, Geordie shouldn't be up there.

DANGERMOUSE: Not like there's much happening down here,
boss.

STEWART: Not the point, Danger.

FREDDIE: And that's another thing I hate about this place. The
wind. When the wind blows, the sand cuts you in two.

DANGERMOUSE: When it gets down your crack, it cuts your
arse in two. My backside's like a peeled –

FREDDIE: Let's not go into your crack, Dangermouse.

DANGERMOUSE: Wouldn't let you near my crack, Fred.

STEWART: Do you boys want to change the record?

FREDDIE: Just having a bit of crack, eh Dange?

STEWART: We're not heading home ourselves just yet.

DANGERMOUSE: First thing I do when I get back to Colly, is go down The Shed and order an ice-cold pint of Stella. Hear B and D companies are out of here tomorrow.

STEWART: So I heard.

DANGERMOUSE: You must be looking forward to seeing Jeannie and the kids, boss?

STEWART: Course I am, Danger.

DANGERMOUSE: Six months must be a long time, when you've got kids like?

STEWART: Isn't she nearly done?

FREDDIE: Heads up, boys, vehicle at two or three K, approaching at speed.

STEWART: Right, into positions boys. Get Geordie, Fred.

FREDDIE: Geordie!

DANGERMOUSE: (*Readying himself.*) One brown raghead, shitting on the wall –

FREDDIE: Geordie, down here now!

DANGERMOUSE: One brown raghead, shitting on the wall –

STEWART: Might be a good time to remind you of the rules of engagement, boys.

DANGERMOUSE: And if one brown raghead should accidentally fall –

STEWART: Three verbal warnings before opening fire.

DANGERMOUSE: It's bang-bang you're dead, fifty bullets in your head.

STEWART: Danger, can it! Geordie, in position, now!

STEWART, FREDDIE and DANGERMOUSE move forward to meet car.

3: THE ESCARPMENT

GEORDIE holds URSULA's satellite dish.

GEORDIE: They're calling me, Ma'am, there's something coming.

URSULA: (*Into sat-phone.*) What's that, Tariq…? (*To GEORDIE.*) Just one more minute, Geordie… (*Into phone.*) Well, if they hadn't had me posted so far back that I can barely see the sand –

GEORDIE: I really must, Ma'am –

GEORDIE places her satellite dish on the most elevated point he can find.

URSULA: Of course, Geordie, you've got to run. You don't have a cigarette before you do?

He throws her a packet of cigarettes and a lighter and moves into position.

Thanks Geordie. No, I can still hear you, but I've lost my aerial. (*Into phone.*) What were you saying?

URSULA lights cigarette.

Yeah, the documentary is coming along great. Lots of interviews, background. In fact, I've got everything except a fucking story.

GEORDIE: Best get down, Ma'am.

URSULA: (*Into phone.*) What's that?

GEORDIE: Car coming full pelt.

URSULA: (*Into phone.*) I know you've got your budget to think of, but I want to stay on until I do have a story, otherwise it will have been an even bigger waste of time and money than it's already been.

GEORDIE: Ma'am!

URSULA: (*Into phone.*) I don't know, something that's closer to the truth than the gung-ho crap the TV channels are putting out –

GEORDIE: Ma'am, there's a car coming full pelt!

URSULA: (*Into phone.*) Listen Tariq, there might actually be something kicking off here. Can you keep the line open and put John on stand-by?

GEORDIE: Ma'am, for the last time –

URSULA: (*Puts out cigarette. Calling.*) I'm down, Geordie. (*Into phone in broadcast tone.*) A white car approaches the checkpoint. It shows no sign of slowing. There are two, no three figures in the car. No. It is now starting to slow… Sergeant McDonald approaches the car. He uses hand gestures and simple English. He is demanding ID. The Iraqis, most probably Bedouin, are getting out. They put their hands on their heads and move away from the car while a soldier searches it… He's found something. The Bedouin are shouting at them. It's money, bundles and bundles of money. They are trying to make a grab for it. The corporal pushes his gun barrel into the driver's chest. The sergeant tries to calm them. He turns and…he starts to come towards me. (*Whispers.*) Putting phone down, Tariq, keep the line open.

Enter STEWART carrying a large bundle of notes.

STEWART: Glad to see you could join us, Geordie. Keep them in your sights. That thing on, Ma'am?

URSULA: No, no reception. Geordie was my aerial.

STEWART: You might be able to help us with this.

He passes URSULA the money.

URSULA: Looks like money, Sergeant McDonald.

STEWART: I can see that, but how much?

URSULA: Big denominations. Over a million. Couple of million.

STEWART: Couple of million?

URSULA: You can count it yourself.

STEWART: But could it be some of Saddam's?

URSULA: Saddam's?

STEWART: The missing millions they said he escaped with.

URSULA: Only insofar as it has his face on it.

GEORDIE: Boss, they're trying to push past Freddie –

STEWART: A minute, Geordie. What do you mean?

URSULA: Iraqi dinars –

GEORDIE: Boss, Freddie's warning them, I'm sure –

STEWART: Then keep him covered. You were saying?

GEORDIE: But boss.

URSULA: Dinars. Two and a half thousand to the dollar. Don't you know the exchange rate?

GEORDIE: That looks like another warning Freddie's given him, boss.

URSULA: A million dinar is worth about four hundred dollars –

GEORDIE: (*Distressed.*) But what should I do, boss?

STEWART: What's an Iraqi doing with over four hundred dollars?

URSULA: Why shouldn't an Iraqi have four hundred dollars?

GEORDIE shoots.

STEWART: What the – ?

More fire off.

(*Rushing forward.*) Cease fire! Cease fire, I said!

URSULA: (*Whispering into sat-phone.*) You getting this Tariq? You still there Tariq? Bastard. Fuck. Minidisc. Where's my fucking minidisc?

She searches in her bag.

> GEORDIE: And Freddie and the Iraqi start to struggle, and you're thinking is that a warning? And Freddie's trying to hold them back? They want their money, like. It's difficult to keep your rifle trained on him with all the pushing and the pulling. And you're thinking how many times is that? Is that three warnings? Then you see it. He's got something in his hand. And then you think, fuck, this is it. (*Pause.*) And it's only afterwards you think, fuck, have I just killed a man?

4: THE VEHICLE CHECKPOINT

DANGERMOUSE and FREDDIE approach the bodies of the shot Bedouins tentatively.

DANGERMOUSE: Hope she got that. Hope that reporter got that one. So my mum can hear what a fucking hero I am.

FREDDIE: Fucking bastard!

DANGERMOUSE: I've got a hard-on, Freddie. All that blatting has given me a hard-on. You got a hard-on, Fred?

FREDDIE: Fucking bastard tried to kill me. Fuck.

DANGERMOUSE: But we got him, Fred, me and Geordie, we got them all. Nice one Geordie. Three nil to the Third Royals.

STEWART arrives.

Eh boss? Three fucking nil.

STEWART: Shut up, Dangermouse.

DANGERMOUSE: Yes, boss.

STEWART: Now could someone please explain what in the name of fuck happened here?

DANGERMOUSE: That one. That one had something. A weapon, like. He went for Fred.

FREDDIE: He tried to fucking kill me.

STEWART: Geordie! Geordie! Get over here, now.

DANGERMOUSE: What's wrong boss?

STEWART: I'll tell you what's wrong, Dangermouse. A few days from going home and hanging up my boots, and I've got a fucking bloodbath to deal with, that's what's wrong.

FREDDIE: He tried to fucking kill me, Stew.

STEWART: Geordie!

FREDDIE: Shall I call Casevac?

STEWART: No. No let's not make this any more complicated than it already is. Right, you lot okay for a start?

Enter GEORDIE.

Geordie?

GEORDIE: What?

STEWART: You okay?

GEORDIE: I don't know.

STEWART: Well either you are or you aren't.

GEORDIE: I don't know, boss, I've never killed a man before.

DANGERMOUSE: Not a virgin soldier any more, kid.

STEWART: Let's have a look at them.

They roll over a body to check for booby trap devices.

FREDDIE: Clear!

DANGERMOUSE: They were armed, boss, I swear.

FREDDIE: Hearts and minds is all very well, Stew, but if it's him or me, it's him.

DANGERMOUSE: Freddie warned them, boss, three times. I counted.

FREDDIE: I did, Stew.

STEWART: Perhaps, but in what language? How did he know you weren't talking about the fucking weather?

Enter URSULA.

URSULA: Sergeant McDonald.

STEWART: Not now, Ma'am, is your phone off?

URSULA: No signal, I said –

STEWART: Good. Now could you please withdraw from the incident site. This is between ourselves, until we find a way of sorting it. That goes for all of us, until we find a way of sorting this out.

URSULA moves back but remains within earshot. They roll another body over to check for booby trap devices. This time something rolls free. They tense up. STEWART inspects the object.

A maglite. A cheap imitation maglite. Is this the weapon you saw, Dangermouse?

DANGERMOUSE: Must have wanted their money real bad to have taken us on with that. Shouldn't mess with the Third Royals, the élite!

STEWART: Maybe he was foolish enough to think that we would behave in a civilised manner.

FREDDIE: Boss, he's still breathing.

DANGERMOUSE: Looks like you're still a virgin after all, kid.

STEWART: Shut up and get the first-aid pack, Dangermouse. Freddie, check the others. See if they're breathing. Let's try and get one thing right.

SAYED: Filoos – [Money.]

STEWART: What's he saying? It's okay. We are going to look after you. Any ID, Geordie?

GEORDIE: Here, boss.

STEWART: Good.

GEORDIE: It's in Iraqi.

STEWART: Ursula!

Enter DANGERMOUSE.

Geordie you take the wound to the stomach. Danger, you take the head.

SAYED: Min fadlika filoos. Alaati saaltoka anha. [Please can you give me the money I asked for.]

STEWART: Someone's coming, she speaks Arabic. Ursula!

URSULA returns.

URSULA: I thought you told me –

STEWART: Well now I need you to translate –

URSULA: But my Iraqi's not –

GEORDIE: It's soaked right through, boss.

STEWART: I need his name. Get another, Geordie. Here are his papers. How's his head Danger?

SAYED: Filoos, al-filoos – [Money, my money –]

STEWART: What's filoos? He keeps saying it.

URSULA: Money. Filoos is money.

FREDDIE returns.

STEWART: Your money's safe. I've got your money here.

FREDDIE: Others are dead, Stew.

STEWART: Right. Danger, I asked how his head was?

DANGERMOUSE: It's a fucking mess, boss. Bits of blood and brain –

STEWART: Just keep the pressure on.

DANGERMOUSE goes to get sick.

STEWART: Freddie, take over.

URSULA: His name's Sayed.

SAYED: Filoos. [Money.]

STEWART: Can you tell him his money's safe.

SAYED: Laah…amoot. [No…die.]

URSULA: He says he's dying.

STEWART: Tell him, Sayed, we're doing our best.

SAYED: (*Very distressed.*) Zawdjati wa ibni. [My wife and my son.]

URSULA: His wife and son, he's saying.

STEWART: What about his wife and son? Danger, tear up some bandages, if you're doing nothing.

DANGERMOUSE does so.

URSULA: Nokoud ila zawdjatika wa atfalika. [Money for your wife and kid.]

SAYED: Filoos el-dem. [Blood money.]

URSULA: Dem? Dem? Blood. Blood money?

SAYED: Aati el-filoos ila al-shekh al masaul an majmooat al-Kuffa. [Give the money to the Sheikh who is in charge of the Kuffa.]

URSULA: Give the money to the Sheikh of the Kuffa.

STEWART: Where do we find him?

FREDDIE: This is soaked through, boss.

STEWART: Dangermouse, more bandages. What's the story, Ursula?

URSULA: I can't say for sure. I think this sheikh has his wife and son.

STEWART: Has them how? As hostages.

URSULA: Perhaps, if this is blood money.

STEWART: Then he must have done something. Ask him why, why they are being held?

SAYED: Katalto ibn akh sheikh al mad, Sheikh al-Kuffa. [I killed the cousin of the Sheikh of the Ma'adan, the Sheikh of the Kuffa.]

URSULA: He killed one of the Kuffa.

SAYED: Madjmouati baou kola abkari wa khorfani min adjilhadihi al filoos. [My people sold all their cows and sheep for this money.]

URSULA: His tribe or people sold everything to raise this money.

STEWART: But how? How do we give it to them?

URSULA: Kayfa naatihiahum? [How do we give it to them?]

SAYED: Kabro a Generals… Al kamar muktamil. [Kabro a Generals…the moon is full.]

URSULA: Kabro a Generals. I've heard of that. The grave of the generals. That's a temple. Kamar is moon. Muktamil. Full moon at Kabro a Generals. Ayna kabro a Generals? [Where is Kabro a Generals?]

SAYED: Fi-altorba al nahshifa fi-jafa. [In the dry marshes in Jafa.]

URSULA: The dry marshes. He must mean the marshes Saddam had drained at Jafa.

STEWART: That was towards Al Amarah. They were heading East.

SAYED: Katalto el-rajul wa…hisab. [I killed the man…debt.]

URSULA: He killed a man, something debt.

SAYED: Wa anta kataltani. Hada hisaboka. [Now you have killed me so the debt is yours.]

URSULA: Now you have killed him, the debt is yours.

SAYED: Ashhado ana la illah illah Allah wa-ana Mohammed rasoul Allah. [I bear testimony there is no god but Allah and Mohammed is his messenger.]

Beat.

STEWART: What did he say? (*Beat.*) Ursula?

URSULA: He said he believes there is no god except Allah and that Mohammed is the prophet of Allah.

FREDDIE: He's dead.

URSULA: Someone give me a cigarette.

> DANGERMOUSE: I don't look, that's how I deal with it. Sounds soft, but bits of skull and blood and all. I'm not soft. I mean, he's the enemy, isn't he? I don't feel anything for him. I hate him, his ugly face, his dirty clothes – I know mine are dirty, but at least I know what it is to be clean – how can you live like that? That's what I tell myself. How can you live like that, you animal? That's what we're doing here, trying to liberate them from living like this. It's not like I really hate him, it's like if I looked, I might, might begin to feel something, how fucking miserable his life, all their lives, are.

5: THE VEHICLE CHECKPOINT

Later. FREDDIE and STEWART stand at the Landrover. STEWART is consulting a map. GEORDIE stands apart in a daze. DANGERMOUSE brings him a cup of tea. URSULA is apart trying to make contact with London on her sat-phone.

FREDDIE: Geordie panicked. He thought they were armed.

STEWART: You signalled to him.

FREDDIE: I was shouting at the raghead to stop trying to push past me.

STEWART: You called on Geordie to fire. You are his superior.

FREDDIE: Well I thought they were armed.

URSULA: (*Into phone.*) Tariq, can you hear me? Damn it, you cut the line, Tariq, in the middle of a live story.

FREDDIE: I warned them Stew, they knew what I was saying.

URSULA: (*Into phone.*) Okay, an Iraqi with four hundred dollars might not be a story –

FREDDIE: What difference does it make anyway?

URSULA: (*Into phone.*) What about three Iraqis shot dead by British soldiers?

STEWART: The world of a difference, Freddie.

FREDDIE: What that's supposed to mean, Stew?

STEWART returns to studying the map. FREDDIE awaits his reply.

URSULA: (*Into phone.*) Well perhaps it's not news to you, but it's what's happening here… What? Three dead Iraqis is old news?

STEWART: Look Freddie, I know what it's like.

URSULA: (*Into phone.*) But three dead Brits and I can have top spot, I suppose?

FREDDIE: Know what what's like, Stew?

URSULA: (*Into phone.*) I'm sorry if the news doesn't fit your agenda.

FREDDIE: Is that what this is really about, Stew?

URSULA: (*Into phone.*) I want to stay on, Tariq, I want to go find this mother and child… Tariq?

The line has gone dead. URSULA tries again.

STEWART: What?

FREDDIE: Her. That girl. Ireland.

STEWART: No Fred, this is about Iraq. It is nothing to do with Ireland. But I do know that if we make it official, by the time the report has gone through to Battalion HQ, the wife and son of that poor bastard Sayed shall be long dead. This is not Ireland, Fred, but one thing I know from there, you do not want this hanging over you. Think about Geordie –

GEORDIE: Didn't you notice, Dangermouse.

STEWART: He's barely eighteen.

DANGERMOUSE: Notice what, kid?

STEWART returns to his map.

GEORDIE: After he died, the silence.

DANGERMOUSE: That's because he'd stopped shouting his head off, hadn't he?

(*Gesturing 'tea' to URSULA.*) Ma'am?

URSULA: In a minute, Danger.

GEORDIE: But there was a sound, Dangermouse.

DANGERMOUSE: Thought you said it was silent.

GEORDIE: It was like wings, or something. Like his ghost rising.

DANGERMOUSE laughs.

DANGERMOUSE: There was no sound, kid. There are no ghosts out here.

FREDDIE: So, what do you propose we do then, Stewart?

STEWART: We've still got two days on patrol. I say we take the money to this Sheikh at this Kabro a Generals. We can do it over land in a night. No one will miss us. (*Pointing to map.*) It can't be too far, it must be in this sector here. Saving his wife and son's life is the least we can do.

FREDDIE: And I say we do it by the book. It's not our job to make moral decisions, Stew. Leave that to the politicians. Let the Ruperts decide.

DANGERMOUSE: Tea's getting cold, lads.

STEWART: Thanks, Danger.

URSULA: (*Into phone.*) Tariq…? (*Wearily.*) Yes I'll hold.

STEWART: Right.

FREDDIE: Right what?

STEWART: I'll call Eeyore at Platoon Headquarters.

FREDDIE: And?

STEWART: I'll put the situation to him. I'll let him decide.

FREDDIE: Good.

Pause.

URSULA: (*Into phone.*) Tariq, listen, I want to go to Kabro a Generals… No, I do not want to pass the details on to the

Jerusalem office, it's my story. I don't care if the embeds have been recalled… I'm going to find that mother and child even if no one else does.

URSULA cuts the line. STEWART will not pick up radio until FREDDIE has left him. At length, FREDDIE goes to DANGERMOUSE and GEORDIE. STEWART turns his back on the other men to speak to Eeyore.

DANGERMOUSE: (*Passing FREDDIE a cup.*) Get that down you, Fred. Wait till you hear, Fred, Geordie's been hearing things. Ghosts.

FREDDIE: You'll get over it, kid.

> STEWART: I see her still. Laughing, always laughing when I see her. In the back window. Green Vauxhall Kadett. Laughing as it pulled away from us. And her hair's long. Black. Curly. Her eyes blue. I can see them. Our eyes met. And as the car starts to pick up pace, moving away from us, she raises her hand, like a cocked gun… The internal inquiry found I'd acted within the rules of engagement. The car had failed to stop. I saw a passenger in the rear make as if to shoot me. I fired a warning shot. The car did not stop. You only have a second to make a decision.

6: THE VEHICLE CHECKPOINT

A helicopter departs.

Later. FREDDIE and DANGERMOUSE are packing and checking the equipment on the Landrover.

FREDDIE: Tacbes?

DANGERMOUSE: Four, check.

FREDDIE: Night-vision gogs.

DANGERMOUSE: One pair, check.

FREDDIE: Mags.

DANGERMOUSE: Twenty…two. And whatever's left in mine and Geordie's. Twelve grenades. Check. Four smoke grenades. Check.

Enter STEWART.

STEWART: How are we doing?

DANGERMOUSE: Nearly there boss.

STEWART: Sooner we make a start, boys, sooner we're home.

FREDDIE: Fucking madness, all of it.

STEWART: With all this kit, what have we got to worry about?

DANGERMOUSE: She didn't look happy when we put her on the heli.

STEWART: Ursula?

FREDDIE: Nosey bitch.

STEWART: Well you don't have to worry about ther anymore, Fred.

FREDDIE: O yeah?

STEWART: I told her, it's between us until it's sorted. Classified information.

DANGERMOUSE: This message shall self-destruct in five, four, three –

STEWART: Eeyore wanted to keep it hush-hush. Besides, the embeds are being recalled. War's over apparently.

DANGERMOUSE performs an exploding message.

FREDDIE: Well that's okay then. Peachy-fucking-creamy. Gimpie, Danger?

DANGERMOUSE: Clean, mean and ready to scream. Pure belt-fed led. Ratatatatatat.

STEWART: How are we on water, Danger?

DANGERMOUSE: Sixty litres. Fifteen each. (*He computes.*) Three days at least.

STEWART: And ration packs?

DANGERMOUSE: Fifteen, which makes fifteen puddings of mass destruction.

DANGERMOUSE takes a pudding, takes a bite then lobs it like a grenade and performs a mock explosion.

Cheer up, Fred, it might never happen.

FREDDIE: How's Geordie getting on?

STEWART: Struggling.

FREDDIE: Fucking madness trying to bury bodies in this sand. Hard as a rock.

STEWART: He wanted to do it.

FREDDIE: Fucking madness, all of it.

DANGERMOUSE: He's spooked. His first time.

FREDDIE: I don't get it.

DANGERMOUSE: I'll give him a hand.

STEWART: That's good of you, Danger.

DANGERMOUSE grabs an RPG from the Landrover.

DANGERMOUSE: (*Exiting.*) Here kid, put those bodies in the car and we'll give them a proper send off.

Exit DANGERMOUSE.

FREDDIE: I mean, we're only a few days from roulement and we've got to cross half the country delivering some raghead money, I just don't get it. Why doesn't Eeyore just call in SIB?

STEWART: Because it will take too long, Freddie, and a woman and a child shall die needlessly. He agreed with me. Play it this way and they'll be giving us medals.

FREDDIE: Fucking Ruperts. Fucking hearts and minds.

STEWART: It's what we're here to do? Leave the country a better place.

FREDDIE: You, maybe.

STEWART: Besides, I thought you wanted to see a bit of action.

Explosion offstage. DANGERMOUSE whoops.

DANGERMOUSE: (*Off.*) Kowabunga!

FREDDIE: Make that eleven grenades.

DANGERMOUSE enters followed by GEORDIE.

STEWART: Right boys, if that's everything…

FREDDIE: Let's get this thing fucking over with.

They get into the Landrover.

7: A STREET IN BASRA

URSULA: How much?

MALEK: But who gave you my name?

URSULA: No one's given me your name. The CNN team pointed you out. They told me you'd worked for them. That you were reliable.

MALEK: You are American?

URSULA: No, British. Irish.

MALEK: Irish?

URSULA: Irish. But I have dollars. So, how much?

MALEK: It's a long way.

URSULA: How long?

MALEK: Hundred and fifty kilometres. And it's dangerous.
    There's a war on, didn't you hear?

URSULA: It's over, according to my editor.

MALEK: Tell your editor I will gladly swap houses with him.

URSULA: You tell me how much you want.

MALEK: Three hundred.

URSULA: Two fifty.

MALEK: And you pay for all petrol, water and comestibles.

URSULA: Done.

8: THE LANDROVER AND THE VOLKSWAGEN

The Landrover. DANGERMOUSE drives, STEWART beside him, GEORDIE and FREDDIE are in the rear.

STEWART: Basra-Baghdad highway coming up, Dangermouse.
    Charlie in mobility told me to take it south ten K to just
    north of Basra, then there's a road east across to the Al
    Amarah road.

DANGERMOUSE: Roger, boss. So what about you Fred?

FREDDIE: What about me what?

DANGERMOUSE: What are you looking forward to when you get back?

FREDDIE: The gasp.

DANGERMOUSE: What gasp's that then, Fred?

FREDDIE: As they lie back on the bed and you slowly, ever so slowly, peel down their stockings and panties. Inch by inch. And they gasp. They always give a little gasp –

DANGERMOUSE: Before they say, I've told you not to wear my underwear you fucking perv!

All except FREDDIE laugh.

FREDDIE: Fuck off!

DANGERMOUSE: Did you hear, boss, Fred likes to wear women's clothes.

FREDDIE: Fuck off Dangermouse, it's the cold air when hits their twats.

DANGERMOUSE: Would you give her one?

FREDDIE: Who?

DANGERMOUSE: Ursula.

FREDDIE: Rather give you one.

DANGERMOUSE: Did you hear that, boss? He wears women's clothes and wants to shag me.

FREDDIE: Fuck right off, Dangermouse.

The Volkswagen. URSULA and MALEK both sit up front.

MALEK: I still do not understand why a pretty lady like yourself would want to go to Kabro a Generals.

URSULA: Because…because I want to help some Iraqis.

MALEK: I wish the world would stop trying to help Iraqis.

URSULA: I'm sorry.

MALEK: The world is sorry, but sorrow does not make the world go round.

URSULA: What does?

MALEK: Dollars.

URSULA: Exactly, and that is why an Iraqi like you would take a pretty lady like me to Kabro a Generals.

MALEK: I am a freedom-loving person, so I must embrace the market. I have nothing else left to embrace.

STEWART: You alright kid?

GEORDIE: Yeah.

STEWART: Don't let it get to you.

URSULA: There are no soldiers in this part of Basra?

MALEK: No need for soldiers here. Mullahs live in this part of Basra. British want the Mullahs on their side. So we can go to Al Amarah this way. But you need to wear niqaab.

URSULA: I beg your pardon?

MALEK: Niqaab, look on the back seat.

URSULA retrieves it.

Put it on.

URSULA: But why on earth – ?

MALEK: Less suspicious.

The Landrover.

STEWART: Wind's picking up.

DANGERMOUSE: You're either frying or freezing in this place.

FREDDIE: Shouldn't we radio in our co-ords, Stew?

STEWART: Eeyore said not to until we've completed the hand-over. Less Ruperts involved at this stage the better.

FREDDIE: Sounds a bit fucked up if you don't mind me saying so, Stew.

STEWART: Well, that's what he said.

FREDDIE: Is it?

STEWART: Yes.

The Volkswagen.

URSULA: If Freddie and Dangermouse could see me now.

MALEK: Who are Freddie and Dangermouse?

URSULA: The dynamic duo. No one. And you, who are you?

MALEK: I am a no one too. I am your rafiq. Desert guide.

URSULA: Should I call you rafiq?

MALEK: No. (*Beat.*) I am Malek.

URSULA: And I am Ursula, Malek. Maybe you'd do an interview for me. Later maybe?

MALEK: No, I shall show you Kabro a Generals, Miss Ursula, I shall translate for you and you shall pay me. Let us keep the relationship colonial.

URSULA: I come from a colony too, remember.

MALEK: Then you shall understand.

The Landrover, largely.

STEWART: According to the Magellan, the desert road Charlie was talking about should be coming up on the left.

URSULA: And why do you have a niqaab in your car?

DANGERMOUSE: Got it.

FREDDIE: Pass us your baccy tin, Stew, mine's in my pack.

URSULA: Is it your wife's? (*Pause.*) Does she not want it any more?

MALEK: No, no she doesn't.

STEWART hands him his tin.

FREDDIE: What's all this crap in here, Stew?

FREDDIE finds newspaper picture.

STEWART: Usual. Codeine tabs, anti-shit tabs, water sterilizing tabs, a baby Absolut –

FREDDIE: And a durex? Hey lads, Stew's feeling lucky tonight.

STEWART: For my gun, Fred.

FREDDIE: It's one of us or a camel.

STEWART: To keep sand out of the barrel.

FREDDIE: To keep sand out of his barrel, eh?! Bags it's Geordie first against the wall. Last in, first –

STEWART: Leave off him, Freddie, you're always having a go.

FREDDIE: But it's okay for Dangermouse to have a go at me?

STEWART: That's different. You can take it.

FREDDIE: Can I? (*Pause.*) And what's this picture, Stew?

STEWART: None of your business.

FREDDIE: This isn't Jeannie.

STEWART: Give me back the tin!

The Volkswagen, largely.

URSULA: Where'd you learn your English, Malek? It's very good.

MALEK: You journalists don't give up.

URSULA: No.

MALEK: I studied in London, British Museum.

URSULA: You're an archaeologist?

MALEK: No, I said, I am nothing.

URSULA: You were an archaeologist, then?

MALEK: I used to work in the Museum here in Basra. Mesopotamian collection. Now, thanks to the Allies, there is no museum and no collection.

DANGERMOUSE: What about you boss?

MALEK: (*Quoting.*) 'How, oh Sumer, are thy mighty fallen. The holy king is banished from the temple. The temple destroyed, the leaders have been carried off into captivity, a whole empire has been overthrown by the will of the gods.' Sumerian lament over the fall of the city of Ur. Four thousand years ago. Even then, Maktub.

URSULA: What's Maktub?

MALEK: What's the point in doing anything? It is the will of the gods.

The Landrover, largely.

STEWART: What about me what?

DANGERMOUSE: What are you looking forward to when you get home?

STEWART: A bath.

DANGERMOUSE: Christ, you and the missus must have an exciting home-life. Still, you must be looking forward to seeing them.

STEWART: Course. The kids especially.

DANGERMOUSE: What about Jeannie?

URSULA: (*To herself.*) Maktub.

FREDDIE: What's that you're writing kid? A bluey to the girlfriend?

GEORDIE: Nothing.

FREDDIE tries to grab GEORDIE's letter.

FREDDIE: 'Dear Mum.' She your girlfriend?

GEORDIE: Leave go, Freddie.

FREDDIE holds GEORDIE back while he reads.

FREDDIE: 'Dear Mum, another letter you probably won't get, because I will have come back safe, but just in case – '

DANGERMOUSE: Leave him be, Fred, he's only a kid.

FREDDIE: What's wrong? Just a bit of in-flight entertainment. 'Sometimes I wonder how many of these letters are written. All the lads writing all they wanted to say to the people they love…' Aw! '…then tearing them up when they get back again.' Sorry, was exaggerating when I said entertainment. 'Where do all the words go? The lads were winding me up about hearing voices out in the desert. In the wind. It really does sound like voices, Mum. Maybe it's all these letters.' (*Pause.*) 'But today was different. Today I killed a man. Two.' Well that's not true because Dangermouse definitely whacked the other two, didn't you Danger?

Silence. STEWART takes the letter from FREDDIE and returns it to GEORDIE.

Jesus!

The Volkswagen.

MALEK and URSULA accelerate.

MALEK: The Al Amarah Road, Miss Ursula.

URSULA: A hundred and fifty K of this and we'll be there by midnight.

MALEK: The last fifty's over desert road. It won't be easy. Saddam had all the tracks destroyed to keep people away.

URSULA: Why?

MALEK: How can we know? We were kept away. Maybe it's not only generals buried there. The soil of Iraq is full of ghosts. Old ones and new ones.

The Landrover.

STEWART: (*Pointing.*) Look, Danger, lights. Must be the Al Amarah road above Basra. Good time, boys, we're making good time. We keep this up and we'll be there by midnight.

The Volkswagen.

MALEK slows.

MALEK: There's something up ahead.

URSULA: Where?

MALEK: There. Cars.

URSULA: It's a road.

MALEK: They're not moving.

URSULA: What is it?

MALEK: Bandits.

URSULA: Shit.

MALEK slows the car.

9: THE AMBUSH

Night-time, off the Al Amarah road. STEWART, FREDDIE and DANGERMOUSE are doing a reccy on foot. DANGERMOUSE wears the night-vision goggles.

FREDDIE: But Danger said it looked like a checkpoint Stew, why pull us over? Why would you be worried about a checkpoint Stew?

STEWART: Shut it, Fred.

FREDDIE: I mean, if it's a checkpoint it would be ours wouldn't it? Our boys?

STEWART: I said shut it Fred. What can you see, Dange?

FREDDIE: I mean HQ has given us the go-ahead, haven't they?

DANGERMOUSE: Two, no three vehicles, both civilian.

STEWART: That's why it worries me, Fred. That's why we are approaching with care.

FREDDIE: They're just having a chat.

DANGERMOUSE: Iraqi style. One with a rifle, two with their hands on their head.

FREDDIE: Raghead on raghead. Leave them to it. Iraq for the Iraqis, I say.

STEWART: Don't call them ragheads, Fred.

FREDDIE: Which fucking side you on, Stew?

DANGERMOUSE: He's only having a bit of fun, boss.

STEWART: We're the ones who let the genie out of the bottle. You heard Eeyore at commencement. If we fail to resolve situations like this one, we shall be deemed to have failed.

FREDDIE: We'll have failed if we get ourselves killed.

STEWART: Then we better not get ourselves killed.

FREDDIE: And it's worth risking our lives for this worthless money?

STEWART: I've told you, Freddie –

FREDDIE: Or is it just a chance for you to play the hero for every sand-nigger with a problem –

STEWART: Freddie, back to the 'rover! Tell Geordie to come here. He can cover us. That's an order.

Pause.

DANGERMOUSE: Boss, they're headed this way.

STEWART: Now Corporal!

Exit FREDDIE.

DANGERMOUSE: Why are they coming this way, boss?

STEWART: He's getting them off the road. To shoot them, most likely.

DANGERMOUSE: What's up with Fred?

STEWART: Don't know, Danger. Where's Geordie?

DANGERMOUSE: (*Looking back.*) On his way.

STEWART: You don't have a problem with this, do you Danger?

DANGERMOUSE: I just follow orders, boss. Hear no evil, see no evil, that's me.

Enter GEORDIE.

GEORDIE: What is it, boss? Why d'you send Freddie back?

DANGERMOUSE: Heads up, they're coming within range.

Enter MALEK and URSULA wearing a niqaab, prodded along by a BANDIT with a rifle. STEWART gestures for the other two to get into position.

BANDIT: Taharek! [Move!]

MALEK: Arjook, ukhuth sayarati. Ukhuth filoosi. [Please take my car, my money.]

BANDIT: Wa yimkin akhuth zawjatuk baa'd? [Can I take your wife too?]

MALEK: Haya moo zawjati. [She is not my wife.]

BANDIT: Wa yimkin tseer zawjati laa'd? [Can she be mine, then?]

BANDIT attempts to pull back URSULA's niqaab. STEWART has moved up behind the BANDIT.

STEWART: Put down the gun and leave the lady alone.

BANDIT: La tatluq, la tatluq! No gun! No gun! Hatha suour tafahum. [Don't fire! Don't fire! No gun! No gun! This is a misunderstanding.]

MALEK: He says it is just a little misunderstanding. (*To BANDIT.*) Uskut. [Shut up.] (*To STEWART.*) It is no misunderstanding. You understand the situation perfectly.

STEWART: Right, let's go back to these peoples' car and sort this out in a civilised manner –

A burst of machine-gun fire. Everyone jumps to the ground. The sound of the Landrover accelarating.

What the fuck!

DANGERMOUSE: That's our gimpie, boss.

STEWART: I know it's our gimpie. What the fuck is it doing firing at us?

DANGERMOUSE: They're getting away with it, boss, they're getting away with our fucking 'rover.

GEORDIE: There must have been more of them, boss.

STEWART: Where's Freddie? What the fuck's happened Freddie?

VOICE: (*Off.*) Irkab! Irkab Uzayr! [Get in! Uzayr!]

The BANDIT gets up.

BANDIT: Al-hamdullilah wa al-shukru lillah. Al-naar li-Beritannia! Al-naar li-Tonee Blair. Al-naar li-George Bush. [Thanks be to Allah. To hell with Britain! To hell with Tony Blair! To hell with George Bush!]

He runs off to join his accomplice in the Landrover. GEORDIE runs off in FREDDIE's direction.

DANGERMOUSE: They're getting away, boss!

GEORDIE: Their cars too.

DANGERMOUSE: They're getting away with all our gear, boss. I can see them boss, let me take them out.

GEORDIE: Should I fire, boss?

STEWART: No. Freddie! Hold fire. You'll blow it sky high. Fuck! Freddie!

The sound of the Landrover tails into the distance. Pause.

10: THE AMBUSH

Off the Al Amarah Road. Moments later.

STEWART: You two okay?

MALEK: Yes, yes thank you, I am okay.

STEWART: And the lady, your wife?

MALEK: Like I told our friend, she is not my wife.

URSULA: (*Removing veil.*) And I ain't no lady.

STEWART: Fuck's sake!

URSULA: Of all the carjacks, in all the world…

DANGERMOUSE: Alright Ma'am?

URSULA: Thanks for the military intervention, Danger. Sorry about the jeep, boys.

DANGERMOUSE / STEWART: 'Rover!

STEWART: We're not all Americans.

MALEK: Not yet.

Enter GEORDIE supporting FREDDIE. He has been hit on the head. GEORDIE sets him down.

STEWART: Jesus Fred, what the fuck…what the fuck happened?

FREDDIE: How should I know, he got me from behind.

DANGERMOUSE: I don't understand where he came from, I scouted the area with the night gogs.

MALEK: The desert is their terrain, they don't need night goggles.

FREDDIE: And who, might I ask, the fuck are you?

MALEK: Malek, pleased to make your acquaintance I'm sure.

FREDDIE: And where the fucking fuck did she come from?

URSULA: Nice to fucking see you too, Fred, nice.

FREDDIE: Jesus, has anyone got any water?

MALEK: There's some in our car. I'll fetch you some.

Exit MALEK.

URSULA: Anyone got a cigarette?

STEWART passes her his tobacco tin.

FREDDIE: I'll take one and all.

URSULA: What's all this?

URSULA takes a condom out of the tobacco tin.

FREDDIE: I'll show you how it works?

URSULA: You should be so lucky.

URSULA passes FREDDIE the tin. Enter MALEK with water.

How's the car, Malek?

MALEK: All present and correct.

GEORDIE: What about the blood money?

STEWART: Got it in my webbing.

FREDDIE: But what about the magellan, Stew? Or the RPGs? Or the gimpie? Or the fucking radio? What about the water, Stew? Or ration packs? I say we radio platoon headquarters now.

STEWART: With what?

FREDDIE: Her sat-phone, that's what.

URSULA: First thing they took.

FREDDIE: He said everything was present and correct.

URSULA: I had the sat-phone in my bag on my lap. First thing they did was go through my bag.

FREDDIE: Fuck!

URSULA: Malek says it's not far.

FREDDIE: What isn't?

URSULA: Kabro a Generals.

FREDDIE: I'm glad to hear it.

STEWART: How far?

MALEK: Eighty kilometres.

FREDDIE: What are you asking him for? Some raghead with a jalopy?

STEWART: Freddie, language.

FREDDIE: Stew, priorities.

STEWART: We have orders to complete the task.

FREDDIE: Do we? I haven't heard them.

STEWART: I gave you them.

FREDDIE: Oh yeah?

STEWART: I relayed them from Eeyore.

FREDDIE: I saw you on the radio, but I only have your word that that is what he said to you, or that you represented the situation to him accurately, or, indeed, that it was Eeyore you were talking to. How can I be sure what you said was true?

STEWART: Because I am your superior officer. Because that is how the army works, chain of command. Didn't anyone ever tell you?

FREDDIE: I don't know anymore, I just don't. Just like I don't know why you've got that picture in your baccy tin.

FREDDIE throws the tobacco tin down. URSULA kneels to retrieve its contents.

STEWART: What picture? What's that to do with anything?

FREDDIE: It isn't Jeannie.

STEWART: What business is it of yours?

FREDDIE: It's the girl from Ireland.

URSULA: What girl from Ireland?

STEWART: Keep out of this.

FREDDIE: The girl he shot dead in Ireland.

STEWART: Freddie, this is not –

FREDDIE: No, Stew, no, that is where you're wrong. You see, you've nothing to be ashamed of, or feel guilty about, we were there to keep the peace and her lot were going around planting bombs and abducting and torturing and murdering us lot. You're a soldier, you did the right thing, you couldn't take any chances.

STEWART: This has no relevance –

FREDDIE: Yes it does, it's completely relevant, because you've gone soft. Like the army. You're a sentimental bastard and you're going to get us all killed.

STEWART: We are not going to be killed. We are going to make the rendezvous and we are going to give this money to the person it was meant for, or a woman and child are going to die.

FREDDIE: And I say you have misled us. I say the platoon commander did not order this. Or at least if he did, you misled him into sanctioning something he never would have if he'd been in full possession of the facts. Whichever, we are out here in the middle of nowhere risking our necks for a lie.

STEWART: How dare you!

FREDDIE: Well then, was this action ordered by Platoon HQ or not?

Pause.

Fucking bastard. Why?

STEWART: Because it's the right thing to do. Because I believe it is the right thing to do –

FREDDIE: To land us without water, food, comms or transport in the middle of the desert?

STEWART: We made a mistake. Geordie made a mistake firing, and Dangermouse –

DANGERMOUSE: But boss –

STEWART: No, Dangermouse, you did, and you made a mistake calling on them to fire, Freddie –

FREDDIE: For fuck's sake, it's a war, Stew –

STEWART: Our war was not with them. And I made a mistake not staying on top of the situation. And, as you have rightly pointed out, Freddie, I've made a mistake like that before and I have had to live with it for a long time. But the Ruperts are not interested in that, they're interested in how it appears. They'd have called us in and had us write reports and would have passed it up the chain of command. And we'd have had debriefings and one-to-ones until the full moon had been and gone and it would have been too late for the woman and her child. But they are not important since they would not have been Allied victims. Intertribal stuff, that's all. And, in time, Sayed's family or people might have been entitled to a pittance of guilt money from the MoD, if they had the perseverance to find out what procedure to follow and where and when to fill in the forms. And the Ruperts would have been satisfied with themselves because justice – fuck justice! – 'the correct procedures' and 'forms' would have appeared to have been done.

FREDDIE: That's what they're there for, to make decisions.

STEWART: No, they are there to pass the buck. One thing they shall never be is to blame. From Eeyore up to Tony fucking Blair. But we are the ones who shall have to live with it.

Pause.

Okay. Okay then Fred, what do you say we do?

FREDDIE: I say we take the car, we drive it back to base camp. Simple as that. That's what I say. What do you say, Danger?

DANGERMOUSE: I mean, like Fred says, boss, if you lied, I mean misled us, knowingly, like, then…I mean…

FREDDIE: Geordie?

GEORDIE: I don't know, Fred.

FREDDIE: We tell them what happened. We say we attempted to rectify the situation, but while doing so we were caught up in another incident where, while saving two civilian lives, we were set upon.

STEWART: I thought you wanted to see a bit of action.

FREDDIE: I've seen enough for one day.

STEWART: You lost your nerve at the VCP.

FREDDIE: Fuck off.

STEWART: You were happy enough to look after the 'rover.

FREDDIE: I followed orders.

STEWART: You were losing it again.

FREDDIE: I got hit on the head.

STEWART: And aren't you forgetting one thing?

FREDDIE: What's that?

STEWART: That's not our car.

URSULA: And it's not going back to Basra.

FREDDIE: We just saved your arse.

URSULA: Thank you very much, and I'm sure that Malek
would let you ride along in the back, for a small fee.

FREDDIE: What if I put my gun to his head?

STEWART: I'll put a gun to yours, Freddie.

FREDDIE: Well, now we know.

DANGERMOUSE: Know what, Fred?

Pause.

MALEK: Three hundred dollars round trip to Kabro a Generals
and you put your rifles in the boot, gentlemen.

FREDDIE: And where are we meant to get three hundred
dollars from?

STEWART: Indemnity money.

DANGERMOUSE: That's meant as a last resort, if we're really
up shit creek.

STEWART: Look down, Danger, you're up to your waist in it,
and I don't see any cash machines.

GEORDIE: I've not talked to my Mum since my step-dad came on the scene. He's the reason I left. I was young. Ran up debts. Credit cards. Longer I'm out here, the more of my debts I can pay off. Don't spend much in the desert. But each time before we go out, I think there must be easier ways of paying off a debt.

Pause. GEORDIE listens to question.

Will I read it to you? (*Uncertain.*) Sure. (*Reads.*) Dear Mum, another letter you probably won't get because I will have come back safe, but just in case...

11: THE VOLKSWAGEN

Near dawn. MALEK drives, URSULA now back in her own clothes, sits in the passenger seat. In the rear sit STEWART, FREDDIE and DANGERMOUSE, while GEORDIE sits squashed across them.

FREDDIE: Move your elbow, Dangermouse.

DANGERMOUSE: Up yours!

FREDDIE: It is up mine, you fat bastard!

DANGERMOUSE: I've got big bones.

FREDDIE: You're a fat bastard.

URSULA: Enjoying yourself, boys?

FREDDIE: Fuck off.

MALEK: Please do not address a lady like that in my car, Mr Freddie.

FREDDIE: What lady?

STEWART: Can you turn on the radio, Malek, a bit of distraction might help.

MALEK turns on radio. An Arabic song is playing.

FREDDIE: Least I don't have Geordie on my knee, little lapdog.

GEORDIE: Fuck off.

FREDDIE: Can't you go any faster Mr Raghead?

MALEK: Yes, if you and your friends would care to step out.

STEWART: Isn't there a shorter route cross-country, over the desert?

MALEK: Maybe in your jeep –

ALL: 'Rover!

MALEK: As you like. But this is Volkswagen Passat, Iraqi edition, tin can on wheels. We must go north on highway and then use desert road.

FREDDIE: What is this shit?

MALEK: This, Mr Freddie, is a very popular song, it is called 'I hate Israel'. He is singing: 'Since the fall of the towers, we are living in a tornado.'

FREDDIE: Raghead bullshit. It's this country I hate –

MALEK slams on the brakes, they are all thrown.

MALEK: You hate this country?

FREDDIE: Steady on, Mr Raghead, we're packed pretty tight in here.

MALEK: Look around you.

FREDDIE: What?

MALEK: What do you see?

FREDDIE: Fuck all, it's barely dawn.

MALEK: What do you see against that dawn? On the horizon?

FREDDIE: Pylons. Electricity pylons.

MALEK: No, Mr Freddie, they are broken electricity pylons, broken because they have been bombed. Look, look, at the side of the road, burnt out cars. How many can we see from here? Five? Six? And I'd swear if you look close enough, you'll find the charred remains of 'ragheads' that even the vultures and the rats won't touch. To remove this monster Saddam, whom you made to keep us in our place, you have bombed us, impoverished us, stood by and let our children die of the most preventable illnesses, starved us physically and intellectually, and then bombed us some more. You have destroyed our country. Take a good look at it, because when I look at its blasted remains, I see you. You reduce a country to rags, and then you call us ragheads.

Pause.

FREDDIE: I meant your turban thing.

MALEK: It's called a keffiyya! I have learnt your language, kindly take the trouble to learn this one word. And it might have escaped your notice, but I am not wearing one. (*Beat.*) I'm waiting.

FREDDIE: What for?

MALEK: An apology.

FREDDIE: Don't push your luck. Remember who's got the gun.

MALEK: Whenever the word liberty is heard, a gun's not far behind.

STEWART: Say it Freddie.

FREDDIE: He can fuck off.

DANGERMOUSE: For fuck's sake, Fred, we don't want to be here all night…

FREDDIE: Right. Sorry. Sorry. If it makes you feel better. Sorry. Fuck.

MALEK: My wife is dead. My daughter is dead. My work strewn to the four winds. My life is dust. Nothing could make me feel better. (*Beat.*) But I shall drive on.

12: THE DESERT ROAD TO KABRO A GENERALS

FREDDIE, DANGERMOUSE, GEORDIE are stretching by the car and passing round a bottle of water. STEWART and MALEK consult the map. URSULA sits apart. The World Service plays on the car radio.

STEWART: Easy on there boys, it's not ours and, besides, we've only got ten litres between us.

FREDDIE: We're meant to have five a day each in this heat.

STEWART: So, take it easy. We'll have to cut across the desert here, Malek.

MALEK: But what about my car, Sergeant McDonald?

STEWART: I'll pay for any damage.

MALEK: With what?

STEWART: When you get us safely back. Hang on.

STEWART turns up the car radio. They all listen.

NEWSREADER: …Mr Blair reacted angrily to the allegation that he had misled Parliament in taking the country to war on a false pretext. He said it was only a matter of time before Saddam's weapons of mass destruction were found. Meanwhile, reports are just coming in from Iraq that a British Army Landrover has been found burnt-out on the Basra-Al Amarah road. There are no signs of any of the occupants or their equipment. It is thought they were on special operations. Sport now, and Patrick Viera's chances of making Wednesday's crucial Premiership decider with Manchester United…

STEWART turns it off.

STEWART: Fuck!

DANGERMOUSE: I know, the Gooners are handing those Manc bastards the title.

STEWART: The 'rover, Dangermouse, that's us.

DANGERMOUSE: But they said it was special ops.

FREDDIE: Only because they've no idea what our 'rover's doing there.

DANGERMOUSE: Hey lads, we're on special ops, we're artists now. Hereford Hooligans. Like Bravo Two Zero. My Mum will be dead proud.

FREDDIE: And that was a fuck-up and all.

URSULA: I need a pee.

FREDDIE watches as she takes her bag and moves away.

STEWART: It's nearly light. We'd best get going. When we're well clear of the road, we'll keep our eyes peeled for a proper LUP. We'll have to lie up in a couple of hours with the heat.

FREDDIE: Who are we hiding from, Stew? Our own lot?

STEWART: The country's still crawling with Fedayeen, and we've got fuck all ammo, Fred.

FREDDIE: And what's the nosey bitch up to now?

DANGERMOUSE: You're trying to cop a look, you are.

FREDDIE: Fuck off!

DANGERMOUSE: You do want to give her one.

FREDDIE: Fuck off I said.

STEWART: You boys pack up.

> *STEWART goes to URSULA who is squatting, trying to make a hurried, whispered phonecall.*

I can't decide whether it's a funny way to take a piss or a funny way to make a call.

URSULA: Is a woman not entitled to some privacy?

STEWART: Not if she's jeopardising the mission.

URSULA: I was just going to let them know I was okay, and where I was and anyway, Sergeant McDonald, you're not on an official mission.

STEWART: Or just plain dropping us in it.

URSULA: And I'm no longer an embed.

STEWART: Every radio signal coming out of this place is being monitored. And with them finding the 'rover, every checkpoint and eagle patrol will be looking for us. You were instructed on your training not to give away positions –

URSULA: To the enemy, not to our own side.

STEWART: It will jeopardise the op nevertheless. And if Freddie finds you've still got your sat-phone, he'll want to call in a heli.

URSULA: I need to let them know I'm safe.

STEWART: You'll be safe, but you'll have no story.

URSULA: The army is not looking for me, Stewart.

STEWART: We are your story.

URSULA: If I don't phone in, I still get to record the story, on my minidisc?

STEWART: Sure.

URSULA: And I'll have yours and the others' full co-operation with interviews?

STEWART: I'll tell them.

URSULA: And publishing rights?

STEWART: Have to talk to my agent about that. (*Beat.*) The book, the film, whatever, it's yours.

URSULA: Right.

STEWART: Now, let's get going, ma'am.

URSULA goes to car, slings her bag and then herself in. MALEK has been trying to start the engine.

What's wrong Malek?

MALEK: Stuck. A stone. And you want to drive off-road in this thing?

STEWART: Well, what are you waiting for lads?

They go to push it. DANGERMOUSE examines the stuck wheel.

DANGERMOUSE: It isn't a stone, boss.

STEWART: What?

DANGERMOUSE: It's a shell. An unexploded shell. American.

FREDDIE: Fucking yanks! Fucking litterbugs!

STEWART: Malek, Ursula, out of the car! Don't ask, get out now. Leave your things. Don't close the doors. Everyone, move away, quickly, carefully, move back. Look where you're going, there might be others.

All except DANGERMOUSE move back.

DANGERMOUSE: I'll grab the guns, boss.

STEWART: Forget the guns, Dangermouse, move away from the vehicle.

URSULA: My sat-phone, Dangermouse, it's in my bag – !

FREDDIE looks at her.

DANGERMOUSE: No problems, Ma'am. I'll risk it for a biscuit.

FREDDIE: Forget about the nosey bitch and move, Dange.

FREDDIE, STEWART and GEORDIE have moved back and off. URSULA stands where the office was in the first scene. DANGERMOUSE has grabbed a bag, the water and four guns. He freezes, visible through the following.

13: THE EDITOR'S OFFICE

FREDDIE is revealed as he was in the first scene. SOPHIE is standing by URSULA.

FREDDIE: Why do I hate you? Who says I hate you?

URSULA: (*Interviewing him.*) You call me a nosey bitch.

FREDDIE: Yeah well…

URSULA: Why, Freddie?

FREDDIE: Because all you lot are interested in is the story. And to make your stories suit your agenda, you have to have goodies and baddies. And the agenda dictates that the army is always painted as the baddy. Yet we didn't choose to be here –

URSULA: You joined the army.

FREDDIE: But I didn't choose this war.

URSULA: You know that the army fights wars.

FREDDIE: I'm only doing this because I was ordered.

URSULA: What is our agenda, then?

FREDDIE: Well, look at yourself. I knew what the story was going to be the minute I met you.

URSULA: And that was? Because I'm a woman?

FREDDIE: I'm not sexist.

URSULA: Because I'm Irish?

FREDDIE: I'm not racist –

URSULA: I report the truth. The facts. What happens.

Exit FREDDIE.

DANGERMOUSE: I got them, I got them all, lads.

DANGERMOUSE slams boot shut, the car explodes.

SOPHIE: Ursula? Ursula?

URSULA: Maybe I'll take that coffee now, Sophie.

INTERVAL

Act Two

1: THE EDITOR'S OFFICE

URSULA sits at the desk with her minidiscs. She is alone. She takes the tobacco tin from her bag and starts to roll a cigarette. She presses play. STEWART appears.

> STEWART: Eighteen, you come home on leave. You're fit. Money's burning a hole in your pocket while your mates are all stoney-broke. All the girls are after you. And you sow your wild oats. You're Jack-the-Lad. You're it. And you get one of them pregnant. So you do the decent thing. I did the decent thing. But then reality kicks in. Off to Germany or Ireland, in my case Ireland, and you're living in this small isolated community, and you are out on patrol all day and she's stuck at home and feels like an extraterrestrial. But the tension of the place and the smallness of the community and the smallness of the babies keeps you tied together and it's not till you get back to England, that you realise that the tension's still there, but it's between you. You realise you were only really kids when you met and that now you've nothing in common. At least I've realised that we have nothing in common.
>
> *STEWART takes photo from pocket.*
>
> My wife, Jeannie.
>
> *STEWART listens to a question. Enter TARIQ. URSULA doesn't see him.*
>
> She still loves me. I think she loves me. Sure she does.

TARIQ: Ah, Ursula –

URSULA jumps and drops the tobacco tin and its contents on the floor. She snaps off the minidisc.

Welcome home.

URSULA: Jesus Tariq!

TARIQ: I'm afraid there's no smoking anywhere in the building. Especially in my office.

URSULA: Lucky I don't smoke then.

She puts the roll-up back in the tin.

TARIQ: Here, let me –

TARIQ picks an item. URSULA takes it from him.

URSULA: Please, I know where everything goes.

Pause.

TARIQ: So, how are you, Ursula?

URSULA: I'm fine.

TARIQ: You're looking well.

URSULA: Am I? You look tired.

TARIQ: I am.

URSULA: Your intern was filling me in.

TARIQ: The lovely Sophie.

URSULA: She seems nice. Smart.

TARIQ: They're all nice and smart. I have a drawer full of lovely Sophies and their nice smart CVs. Luckily. Got to replace them every three months before we have to pay them a proper wage. Where is she?

URSULA: Coffee.

TARIQ: Ah, the new truck, did you see it? Espresso, macchiato, ristretto, the works.

URSULA: Was it bad?

TARIQ: You know what they're like, lawyers. They love the chance to put us in our places.

TARIQ looks at SOPHIE's disc log.

Hasn't she finished it yet?

URSULA: My fault, I interrupted her. Is Gilligan's source not sound then?

TARIQ: Excuse me?

URSULA: The 'sexing up' claim.

TARIQ: Not my source. Not my story, I'm glad to say.

URSULA: But now your problem?

TARIQ: You don't give up!

URSULA: A good journalist…

TARIQ: I understand from my colleagues that their source is reliable.

URSULA: But do you think it is?

TARIQ: What I think is neither here nor there. I have no evidence that leads me to believe that my colleagues are anything other than committed to fairness, accuracy, and impartiality in all their reporting.

URSULA: But you do suspect there's an agenda?

TARIQ: Nor is what I suspect either here or there.

URSULA: You've been with the lawyers too long.

TARIQ: And you in the field. What I do know, Ursula, is we've got to be careful, and some of us more than others.

URSULA: You mean...you?

TARIQ: From now on you must call me Derek. (*Beat.*) I'm joking, Ursula. Good God, things have not got that bad yet. And I know myself to be crucial to the station's equal opportunities figures if not their listenership figures. And here comes the lovely Sophie –

Enter SOPHIE.

SOPHIE: Sorry about the wait, Ursula, long queue. Getting on for lunchtime. Oh, Tariq. Did you – ?

TARIQ: No thanks. No coffee. Doctor's orders. Heart.

SOPHIE: Your heart Tariq?

URSULA: You have one?

TARIQ: Starts racing even when I am sitting still. Don't worry ladies, I am assured it's not serious. Worst part of it is the coffee deprivation. I actually have dreams about coffee. They border on the erotic. But it's not me we're here to talk about, but the brilliant Ms Ursula Gunn and her adventures with Her Majesty's Third Royal Fusiliers in the deserts of the further Euphrates. And these are the recordings? Must be very good. Some one from 'army media relations' has been on the phone every day since you got back looking for them. A major, no less. Though I suspect the interest might derive from the Special Investigation Branch.

SOPHIE: Perhaps I should be –

URSULA: What did you say to them?

TARIQ: That's why I had Sophie log them. No, stay Sophie. We've nothing to hide, do we?

URSULA: What did you say to them, Tariq?

TARIQ: Nothing. I contrived to be occupied with pressing business whenever he called. But I cannot contrive to be so occupied forever, much as our lawyers would wish it so.

TARIQ picks up a minidisc.

Sorry I haven't managed to listen to them yet. As I said, occupied with pressing business. Can you give me a taste of what we've got? See what the story is.

URSULA: The real story?

TARIQ: What other story is there?

URSULA: The one the MoD have told the world.

TARIQ: Well then…

TARIQ loads minidisc.

DANGERMOUSE appears.

DANGERMOUSE: Why do they call me Dangermouse?

TARIQ: Dangermouse?

SOPHIE: Private Darren Williams.

DANGERMOUSE: You remember Dangermouse, the cartoon? "'Dangermouse you saved the world!' 'It's only a job, really.'" I used to watch it as a kid. I'm not one of those sad bastards who watch all the stuff they used to watch when they were kids when they're grown up, mind. But when I got my first pay packet from the army, me and the lads went out on the town in Colly, Colchester, and had a few bevvies. Got really shit-faced to tell the truth. Went to this tattoo shop. To get '3RF' tattooed on our arms. I must have been talking about Dangermouse or something – you know the way you talk about kids telly when you're pissed – because next morning I woke up with this tattoo on my arm. The lads thought it was a real laugh. First I was hacked off about it, but now I've got used to him, my lucky charm.

2: THE DESERT ROAD TO KABRO A GENERALS

The aftermath of the explosion. The ground is covered with the debris of the car. DANGERMOUSE lies surrounded by the others.

FREDDIE: His arm, fuck!

GEORDIE: It's ripped right off.

STEWART: Dangermouse, can you hear me?

DANGERMOUSE: Got the guns, boss.

STEWART: Shit, Dangermouse.

DANGERMOUSE: And your sat-phone, ma'am.

URSULA: Ursula, Dange.

FREDDIE grabs the remains of URSULA's bag and phone.

FREDDIE: Give me that sat-phone, give me that fucking sat-phone, I'm calling a fucking heli.

URSULA attempts to recover her bag, while FREDDIE tries phone.

URSULA: My bag, my recordings!

FREDDIE: It's fucked! Fuck! You had it all along and now it's fucking fucked!

DANGERMOUSE: I had them. In my hand.

STEWART: Don't talk, Dange, I'm going to try a tourniquet.

DANGERMOUSE: ...Down the shed, an ice-cold pint of Stella...

FREDDIE: You mad bastard, Dangermouse.

DANGERMOUSE: Mad, bad and dangerous to know.

STEWART: Don't worry, he's only passed out.

FREDDIE: Don't worry?

STEWART: I mean he's not dead.

FREDDIE: Yet. He's dying, Stew.

STEWART: I know.

FREDDIE: He's completely fucked.

STEWART: I know.

FREDDIE: What the fuck do we do now, Batman?

STEWART: I need to think.

MALEK: And I'm afraid now you do owe me a new car, Sergeant McDonald.

FREDDIE: Shut up about your fucking car!

URSULA: It was because I shouted, it was because… .

FREDDIE: You shut the fuck up too! What's it to be, Stew?

STEWART: We lie up for the day, see how Danger does, grab some gonk if we can. Try and lose as little water as possible. This evening, if Danger doesn't make it, we strike out for the North East across the desert to Kabro a Generals.

FREDDIE: You're not seriously still thinking – ?

STEWART: It's not more than twenty-five clicks as the crow flies.

FREDDIE: It's not more than ten klicks back to the main road. We take our chances, flag something down.

STEWART: Whatever. In this heat we'll have to lie up till evening. We can decide then.

> GEORDIE: When you go down the Job Centre and ask about careers in the army, they show you tanks rolling through woodlands and guys patrolling through trees with twigs sticking out of their helmets. They don't show you what it looks like when your mate's arm's been blown off, and you've shot a man. And you've no water or bandages, or nothing, and haven't slept all night. They don't tell you that all your actions have consequences for someone.

Exit GEORDIE.

3: ON THE DESERT ROAD TO KABRO A GENERALS

Later, mid-day, blisteringly hot. URSULA alone in the shade of a rock, she is making a recording onto her minidisc.

URSULA: It was my fault, Dominic, my stupid fault. I shouted at him to get the sat-phone and my discs. It's a reflex. I'm programmed that way. The story is all that counts. Just like he's programmed to obey orders. I shouted to him to get my things, Dom, he heard and obeyed. Remember we used to sit on the sofa together after school, like two peas in the pod, watching 'Dangermouse', and now he's lying on the red sand, his blood draining from the stump of where his arm once was. Jesus, Dom, what price the truth?

FREDDIE has entered quietly behind her.

FREDDIE: What you doing over here, Ma'am?

URSULA: Jesus, Freddie, you made me jump.

FREDDIE: Dangerous over here. Could be more cluster bomb shells, or mines.

URSULA: Couldn't sleep, scorpion in my shoe. Didn't you feel like sleeping? How is he?

FREDDIE: How do you think? Stew gave him some codeine pills and a baby Absolut when he came round.

Pause.

URSULA: I know what it's like for you, Freddie.

FREDDIE: Do you? How's that then?

URSULA: I lost my brother. Dominic.

FREDDIE: To an American cluster bomb shell?

URSULA: No, to an RUC bullet. An accident. I mean, they're not even meant to kill anyone, rubber bullets. Nor the police, they're not meant to kill either.

FREDDIE: These things happen.

URSULA: He was going to a school disco.

FREDDIE: Sometimes you've got to make snap decisions. Mistakes can be made.

URSULA: But there was no inquiry into the mistake. They didn't even apologise. They just told lies about him, what he was doing, who he was friends with, to cover up their mistake.

FREDDIE: Sometimes the truth must be sacrificed to a greater end.

URSULA: No, the truth must be known. That's why I became a journalist. To tell things as they really are. It's the least we owe those upon whose suffering our world is built.

FREDDIE: You must be happy then.

URSULA: Happy?

FREDDIE: This must be like revenge.

URSULA: Revenge?

FREDDIE: Seeing us suffer.

URSULA: I'd never wish that on anyone –

FREDDIE: Well, you've got your story now.

URSULA: I've told you –

FREDDIE: Probably got it running now.

URSULA: Only because you interrupted –

FREDDIE: Danger lost his arm, most probably his life for this gear –

FREDDIE takes the minidisc player.

URSULA: I'll turn it off. Don't touch it.

FREDDIE grabs her arm.

Don't touch me, Freddie.

FREDDIE: I've been watching you all along.

URSULA: Freddie, don't, we're in trouble enough.

FREDDIE: (*Forcing her down.*) Whose fault is that? Stew's lost it. I wanted to turn back, but you gave Stew an out, saying they'd stolen your sat-phone. Where was the truth there, truth-seeker?

URSULA: Freddie – !

FREDDIE: The others would have come with me, but you twisted Stew round your little finger. Standing with your knickers round your ankles, waving your cunt at him. And then you shouted to Dangermouse to get your stuff. You're the one who's made mistakes. Danger's biggest problem is that he's a decent guy. It gets in the way of his professionalism.

URSULA: Freddie, I'll scream.

FREDDIE: No you won't, because I'm sick of listening to you.

FREDDIE puts his hand over her mouth, then gags her and snaps plastic cuffs on her.

Just playing at being a soldier. This is war. The genie from the bottle.

(*Sings.*) We shall overcome, we shall overcome...

FREDDIE unzips his flies, through a barrage of kicks he tries to pull URSULA's trousers off. Enter GEORDIE. He moves up behind FREDDIE. URSULA stops thrashing. FREDDIE looks around. GEORDIE cracks FREDDIE in the side of the head with his rifle butt. He takes off URSULA's gag.

What the fuck – !

URSULA: Bastard! Filthy fucking bastard!

FREDDIE: My ear! My fucking ear! What the fuck you doing spying on me?

URSULA: Bastard!

FREDDIE: It's between me and her.

GEORDIE: Didn't look that way to me, Corporal.

FREDDIE: You fuck off you little shit, or I'll have your balls for breakfast.

GEORDIE: I'm afraid I can't do that, Corporal.

FREDDIE: You follow that soft bastard McDonald like a dog across the desert, and now you won't obey me?

GEORDIE: Sergeant McDonald is trying to do the right thing.

FREDDIE: Since when is it your job to think what's right and what's not? It's about obeying orders, and I've given you an order.

GEORDIE: And I'm afraid I can't obey you, Corporal.

STEWART has entered, followed by MALEK.

FREDDIE: (*Going for GEORDIE.*) You little – !

STEWART: Stand down, soldier!

URSULA: Keep him away from me, Geordie.

FREDDIE: You don't have the balls, Stew. You're all hearts and minds, and no balls.

STEWART: Don't push me, Fred, normal rules don't apply any more. You've made sure of that.

Pause. At length FREDDIE puts his hands up. GEORDIE relieves him of his gun.

URSULA: Keep him away from me.

STEWART: Geordie, take Ursula into the shade and look after her.

Exit GEORDIE with URSULA.

MALEK: So, this is the liberation you bring us?

STEWART: Please Malek, not now.

MALEK: The actions of lovers of freedom. Skham wijih. Skham wijih, Sergeant McDonald.

Pause. FREDDIE sneers at STEWART and walks off in the opposite direction to GEORDIE and URSULA.

STEWART: What is skham wijih, Malek?

MALEK: During the last war, on the retreat from Kuwait, Saddam ordered the army to set fire to all the oil wells as an act of defiance. A final 'fuck you' to the Allies. But true to Iraqi luck, the wind began to blow from the south and the air of Iraq became black with burnt oil particles. Our cars, our houses, our roads and, if you dared to venture out, your face went black. Skham wijih. Black faced. Shamefaced. Shame on us. Be careful, Sergeant McDonald, the wind is picking up.

Exit MALEK, enter GEORDIE.

GEORDIE: Dangermouse is dead, boss.

STEWART: And we don't even have an RPG to give him a proper send off.

4: THE DESERT ROAD TO KABRO A GENERALS

Late afternoon. URSULA is recording MALEK. This interview takes place within the real time of the scene.

MALEK: The day the bomb came was my daughter's birthday. I had saved. Saved a whole year. She had set her heart on a white silk dress. Nothing we could do could persuade her to change her mind. She wanted to look like an angel that she had seen in a book of Christian Art I had bought in London. And, as Mr Bush threatened war, and the dinar fell lower and lower, I had to save harder and harder to buy it. We ate less. We would not drive, but walked everywhere. And, at last, I was able to buy her dress. She looked like an angel in it. I went to work at the Museum happy. That same day, the Allies started what they called pre-war bombing in Basra. The Tree of Adam was bombed. It's what Christians call the Tree of Life. It had stood in Basra since before time and was supposed to be guarded by Allah and have healing powers. My home was bombed that day too. My daughter had wanted the dress to be an angel to go to heaven in.

URSULA: Is that why you continue with us?

MALEK: What do you mean?

STEWART: For your daughter. To save the Bedouin's wife and child, as a kind of compensation.

MALEK: Compensation? Why do all your English words that are to do with the most important things like heart and soul come from the language of the shopkeeper? Compensation? Redemption? Recompense? Saving? Nothing could compensate me for the loss of that dress, Sergeant McDonald.

URSULA: Why do you continue with us then?

MALEK: Business.

Enter GEORDIE.

There is no language now but the language of the market. The new Iraq will be a knockdown shop for the West. And I am nothing but a shop assistant. (*Beat.*) And I said I wasn't going to talk to you. That will be another twenty dollars you owe me.

STEWART: Any sign, Geordie?

GEORDIE: No, his gun's gone. And one of the water bottles.

STEWART: He's bugged out. He's headed back towards the Basra road. He'll fry in this.

GEORDIE: Shouldn't we go after him?

STEWART: No. He's made his choice. I made mine. I'll repay this debt.

GEORDIE: What about us? We need five litres of water each day in this heat.

STEWART: We wait till evening. Conserve energy. We walk to Kabro a Generals then.

MALEK: It will not be a stroll in the park, and the wind is really picking up.

GEORDIE: What about maps, boss? They were in the car.

STEWART: We still have the stars, kid. Don't they teach anything in basic training these days? How they used to do it in ancient times, isn't that right Malek?

MALEK: Bedouin still do. The sky is a map. A reflection of the world.

STEWART: And tonight we have a full moon to walk by.

5: ACROSS THE DESERT

Night. Walking.

GEORDIE: How far do you reckon we've done, boss?

STEWART: Ten klicks. Good progress.

Enter MALEK.

MALEK: My shoes are falling to pieces, Sergeant McDonald.

STEWART: How are you doing, Ursula?

URSULA: I'll outlive you all.

STEWART: Let's hope they wait for us.

MALEK: Who?

STEWART: The Kuffa, the Sheikh.

GEORDIE: This is the last of the water, boss.

STEWART: Bastard, Freddie! Don't worry, we'll find some.

MALEK: There used to be water here. This used to be marshland. All these wadis were waterways. Then Saddam dammed up the Euphrates. We will be lucky to find a cup of water.

STEWART: But people still live here? The marsh Arabs?

MALEK: Ma'adan.

STEWART: And the Kuffa, they are Ma'adan?

MALEK: If they are from around here, yes.

STEWART: Ursula says you know about Kabro a Generals. She says it's some kind of temple.

MALEK: Late Babylonian, you call Hellenistic. Another Western invasion.

STEWART: Who were the Generals?

MALEK: Greeks. They led an army of mercenaries here to the deserts of ancient Babylonia. They were in the pay of Cyrus, the pro-Western pretender to the throne of Persia. Even then the West tried regime change.

STEWART: Did they succeed?

MALEK: Cyrus died on the first day of the first battle. The Greek army found themselves without a cause to fight for, lost in the deserts, surrounded by hostile tribes. The Greek generals sent word to the Persians that they were now willing to negotiate. But those sneaky deceitful Easterners tricked them.

STEWART: So they killed them and buried them at Kabro a Generals?

MALEK: The generals had first tried to overthrow the leadership, then they tried to make peace with it. The Persians were not stupid. They realised this to be the hypocrisy it was, so they cut off their heads and had those severed heads displayed there as a sign.

STEWART: A sign of what?

MALEK: The severance between the head and heart at the core of your Western Civilisation.

GEORDIE: What about the other Greeks? The soldiers?

MALEK: Without their generals, they instituted a democracy amongst themselves. They marched home through Kurdestan and Turkey to the Mediterranean shore: 'Thalassa! Thalassa!' Of course, seventy years later the Persian Empire fell to some Greek named Alexander.

STEWART: Alexander the Great?

MALEK: Perhaps in the West he is called great. We think of it more as arrogance. He set up a temple to those generals. In his version of the truth, they became early martyrs in the civilisation of the barbarians. So, what was a sign of treachery to the East, was a shrine to heroism in the West. The wind is picking up.

GEORDIE: I can't see the stars any more, boss.

STEWART: It's cloud.

MALEK: It's not cloud, Sergeant McDonald, it's sand. We must stop.

STEWART: We must keep going. Tonight is the full moon.

MALEK: If we don't stop now, we shall all die.

Pause. Wind.

STEWART: It's blowing from the south-west. Over there, that wadi bank, some hollows. Grab one each. Ursula, come with me.

Wind.

6: THE CAVE

URSULA and STEWART huddle by the light of a torch.

URSULA: They're drawings. It's a cave. Someone lived here.

STEWART: No one lived here. It's the bank of a wadi.

URSULA: Sheltered here then. Look, it's some kind of human figure, but he's got bull's horns.

STEWART: The sand's getting in on you, keep tight to the wall.

URSULA: What about Freddie?

STEWART: He's younger and fitter than me. He had less ground to cover. We can hope. (*Beat.*) I'm sorry, Ursula, about Freddie.

URSULA: Don't. Don't say anything.

Silence, apart from the wind.

Why are you doing this, Stewart? Are you doing it as a kind of compensation?

STEWART: Maybe.

URSULA: Do you actually want to go home?

STEWART: Of course I do.

Beat.

I don't know. Perhaps not quite yet.

URSULA: Is it because of that girl in Ireland? The newspaper cutting. The one Freddie was talking about. Is she the reason?

Pause.

STEWART: I see her laughing, still, always laughing when I see her. In the back window, green Vauxhall Kadett.

Laughing as it pulled away from the checkpoint. And her hair was long. Black. Curly. Her eyes, blue. I could see them. And as the car starts to pick up pace, moving away from us, she raises her hand. And we've been on stag four, five hours, and this is the middle of the night, and I'm tired and twitchy. And she points her index finger and forefinger at me like a gun. She cocks it. And I can see her lips mouthing: 'Bang, bang,' …and I am full of rage. Being where I am and what I am. I close my eyes to calm myself. And when I open them the glass has shattered. And the car is screeching to a halt and jolting forward and rolling back and she is coming out through the shattered back windscreen like, like an avenging angel, still smiling even though there this hole in her head. (*Beat.*) There's not a day goes by I don't see her smiling face and she is saying: 'Bang, Bang, you're the one.' And I am the one. I miss her as if I loved her. Or as if I were dead and it was my life I missed.

Beat.

URSULA: I lost my brother, Dominic. RUC shot him. I still talk to him. How are you doing Dominic? You won't believe where I am, Dominic. The middle of a sandstorm with a fucking squaddie, Dom. (*Laughs.*) Everything decent I've ever done is because of him. Every place I've not had the courage to go, he has held my hand and walked with me. In the valley of death, no evil shall I fear. Even here, now, with you – (*Beat.*) Is this maktub?

STEWART: Maktub?

URSULA: Written by the hand of God. Stewart?

STEWART: What is it Ursula?

URSULA: It's just that I think I'm going to pass out, Stewart. Hold me, hold me in your arms.

He does so.

7: THE DESERT

Early morning, April 17th 2003. GEORDIE, URSULA and STEWART dust themselves down.

STEWART: He's dead or bugged out.

URSULA: I can't believe Malek would have left us.

GEORDIE: He was just along the bank of the wadi.

STEWART: What wadi? The sandstorm's changed the whole landscape. He's gone. He didn't owe us anything.

URSULA: But we owed him a lot. He said it was just business, but he wanted to see it through.

STEWART: Whatever, we can't stay here.

GEORDIE: But what if he's buried, boss.

STEWART: Then we'll never find him.

GEORDIE: But the deadline's passed, boss.

STEWART: Maybe the Kuffa never made it to the rendezvous either with the sandstorm.

URSULA: Christ, I need water.

STEWART: We've got to get moving, it's our only hope.

URSULA improvises a keffiyya.

GEORDIE: What are you doing, Ursula?

URSULA: Making a Keffiyya. The sun will burn us alive.

STEWART: Good idea. Get to it, kid.

They do so.

GEORDIE: If Freddie could see us now! A bunch of ragheads!

They begin to walk. They switch between the direct address of the interviews and dialogue with each other.

> GEORDIE: Nineteen hours a man can go in the desert without water.

> STEWART: We were walking for what seemed like forever along the floor of the wadi. It was once a river, now it was a river of sand.

> GEORDIE: The mirages start normal. Like on a hot day on a tarmac road, a flat stretch seems to shine.

> STEWART: It's never still, the desert. It moves. It is a living thing. Not just when a sandstorm blows it every which way, but even in the stillest moment of the hottest day, it's shifting all the time, under the light. And out of the light and the shadows you start to see the domes of mosques and walls of fortresses, towers and minarets, cities –

> GEORDIE: Ancient cities made of sand which crumble as you reach out to touch them –

> STEWART: As if a natural disaster –

> GEORDIE: Or a bomb or something had sucked out all life and left no explanation.

> STEWART: A man can go nineteen hours in this desert without water. Then his eyes begin to fill with light.

GEORDIE: How far, boss?

STEWART: How long've we been walking?

GEORDIE: Two, three hours.

STEWART: A fair distance, kid. We've done a fair distance. Eight, nine K. We can't be that far.

URSULA: What's that, Stewart?

STEWART: Where? I can't see clearly.

URSULA: Up ahead. In the sand.

GEORDIE: Tracks.

STEWART: Do you both see them?

URSULA: Yes. Can't you?

> STEWART: Can you have collective mirages? Perhaps
> if people want the same thing badly enough.

GEORDIE goes to inspect.

GEORDIE: Footprints.

URSULA: Perhaps they're Malek's.

GEORDIE: There's more than one set.

STEWART: Bedouin.

URSULA: Two sets. Three sets.

GEORDIE: Two large, one smaller. (*Beat.*) What is it, boss?

STEWART: Stewart, call me Stew, kid. They're ours.

GEORDIE: You mean…?

STEWART: It's circular, the wadi. I don't know which way we
are facing any more. I am surrounded by sun. My eyes are
full of blinding light.

> STEWART: Then I saw ghosts: a Bedouin sleeping
> against a tree…

GEORDIE: It's just a rock, boss.

> STEWART: And later. (*Blindly squinting.*) Two children
> running up that hill. Tom and Ella. My kids.
> Jeannie not far behind them.

STEWART: If I call do you think they'll come? Jeannie! Jeannie! She's come to find me. All this way. And we'll talk, and it will be okay.

URSULA: It's okay, Stew.

STEWART: Or maybe it's the woman and child I must save. If only I could reach them, but they keep moving away from me.

GEORDIE: They're the shadows of the vultures overhead. That's all it is, boss.

Time passes. GEORDIE laughs.

STEWART: What are you laughing at, kid?

GEORDIE: I was just thinking, my dad, my real dad died of drink, that's how my mum puts it. And here am I dying for want of one.

> STEWART: Can you have a collective mirage? Perhaps if people want the same thing badly enough. Or fear the same thing badly enough.

GEORDIE: What's that up there?

STEWART: I cannot see, Geordie, I cannot see.

GEORDIE: Ursula?

URSULA: Looks like a tree.

STEWART: You both see it? There must be water. Dig! Dig!

GEORDIE: It looks dead.

URSULA: There's something tied to it.

GEORDIE: It's a man. Hey! Hey!

URSULA: He's not moving.

STEWART: Another mirage.

GEORDIE: No, there is a man. A man tied to a tree. We both see him. Hey!

GEORDIE is making to run to him as best he can.

URSULA: Stop Geordie.

GEORDIE: Why?

URSULA: Because he has no eyes…pecked out by the vultures.

GEORDIE squints, then falls to his knees.

What is it, Geordie?

GEORDIE: It's Freddie. And he's been nailed, not tied.

STEWART: It can't be.

GEORDIE: It is, I swear. And he's been beaten and cut. It's the Fedayeen, they found him and they've taken it out on him: Saddam, the war, the whole crapness of it all, all out on him.

URSULA: It's not Geordie, I promise you, it's not him.

GEORDIE: They've crucified him and left him in the sun to burn.

URSULA comforts GEORDIE.

URSULA: It's okay, Geordie –

GEORDIE: They're following us, boss, they'll get us too.

URSULA: They're not, we're going to be okay, Geordie.

GEORDIE: They will, I know they will.

STEWART: Don't lose it on me now, kid. You're playing a blinder. We need to keep it together until we find water.

GEORDIE: We're not going to find water.

STEWART: We are, and the woman and the child will be there. And they will be okay. And we will be okay.

GEORDIE: The woman and the child are dead and we are going to die.

Silence.

> STEWART: And then it's too difficult to even talk. My tongue and throat swelled up. It was difficult to even breathe. I was slowly suffocating. (*Beat.*) Can you have a collective mirage?

> GEORDIE: At one point we ran down the side of a dune, throwing off our kegs, to jump into the white horses breaking on the sandy shore.

> STEWART: And later, somewhere on the floor of a wadi, we lay down to die.

> *They walk until they can walk no more. The light and the sound of insects intensifies. It becomes the sound of bees.*

> GEORDIE: It was then we heard him. And the sound of…insects –

STEWART: Hello! Hey! Who is it?

URSULA: I can't say. He's got the sun behind him.

STEWART: Help us. Help us please! Why don't you shout?

GEORDIE: His head, boss.

STEWART: What about his head?

URSULA: It's the head of a bull.

GEORDIE: And his beard, his beard is made of swarming bees. What the hell is it, boss?

STEWART: The genie from the bottle.

GEORDIE: And he's laughing. And he has a club, like a small cedar tree, and he's striking the ground with it. And...

STEWART: What?

STEWART is the only one standing and therefore the only one who cannot feel the water.

And what?

GEORDIE: Water.

STEWART: It's another mirage.

URSULA: No, it's real, it's coming up through the ground. Look, water, streams of it. The desert is filling up with water.

STEWART: It can't be. How?

GEORDIE: It is a fucking genie, boss. It's a fucking miracle.

They scrape water from the ground into their mouths. GEORDIE and STEWART start splashing each other like kids.

8: THE RIVERS OF BABYLON

Later.

URSULA: How does a desert fill up with water?

GEORDIE: A fucking miracle.

STEWART: However it did, it did. But now it's getting on for evening. The stars will be out soon. Let's fill the bottles and move on.

URSULA: We're a day late.

STEWART: Perhaps the sandstorm delayed them too. We can only try.

GEORDIE: Boss?

STEWART: What now?

GEORDIE: Four-wheeler. Coming from the North.

STEWART: You imagining things again, kid?

GEORDIE: You still blind, boss? Could be the same ones that did for Freddie.

Car approaches.

STEWART: We don't know what happened to Freddie. (*Beat.*) But cover me anyway.

GEORDIE: My gun's fucked. It won't fire shit.

STEWART: They don't need to know that.

Car stops off and doors open.

MALEK: (*Off.*) Miss Ursula! Sergeant McDonald, Geordie –

STEWART: Malek. Put the gun down, Geordie, it's Malek. It's Malek!

Enter MALEK followed by a Marsh Arab.

STEWART: Another miracle. But how, Malek?

MALEK: Business. I have come to find you. I want my new car.

GEORDIE: But we looked for you. After the sandstorm.

MALEK: I was buried. When it was over, I couldn't find you. I walked north. These Ma'adan found me and took me to their mudith. They gave me food and drink then we set out to look for you. I said you'd reward them. Buy them all cars.

STEWART: Jesus I will, I fucking will. But the water, where did all this water come from? Or was that written by the hand of Allah too?

MALEK: No. Not God. Just Iraqis.

URSULA: But how?

MALEK: When news of the fall of Baghdad reached Ma'adan further north, they begged borrowed and stole any bulldozer, tractor, horse or camel to pull down the dams that Saddam had built across the Euphrates. For the last few days that water has been filling up the wadis. Now, our Ma'adan friends here wish to show you hospitality, get you cleaned up and offer you something to eat.

STEWART: Tell them thank you but we must push on to our rendezvous at Kabro a Generals.

The Marsh Arab kneels.

URSULA: Why's he on his knees?

MALEK: He is saying he will divorce his wife if you do not accept his hospitality.

STEWART: Please explain to him why we must hurry.

MALEK: Sergeant McDonald, the woman and child are okay. He sent word to the Kuffa. You will meet tomorrow. Now you must rest. Come, come.

STEWART and GEORDIE follow MALEK and the Marsh Arab off. URSULA remains.

9: THE EDITOR'S OFFICE

TARIQ: Some good stuff in there.

URSULA: This is just a rough outline.

TARIQ: And those last interviews?

URSULA: Stewart and Geordie?

TARIQ: The hallucinations, when did you make them?

URSULA: That night, at the Marsh Arab's hut.

TARIQ: And you've got some stuff from the next day? From the rendezvous?

SOPHIE: Here they are, Tariq.

TARIQ: Thanks, Sophie.

SOPHIE: There's not much.

URSULA: That's all there was.

TARIQ loads minidisc.

10: KABRO A GENERALS

GEORDIE, STEWART and MALEK in the temple.

STEWART: The grave of the Generals!

GEORDIE: It's cold in here.

STEWART: Makes a change.

GEORDIE: Gives me the willies.

STEWART: That's the smell.

GEORDIE: It's minging.

STEWART: What's the time, Geordie?

GEORDIE: 0800, boss.

STEWART: Should be here by now.

MALEK: Maybe they were held up at a vehicle checkpoint?

STEWART: Maybe you should get a job on the new Iraqi comedy channel.

GEORDIE: Boss, I found something here. Writing.

STEWART: Ursula. You might want to catch this for posterity, Urs.

Enter URSULA.

URSULA: Coming. Christ what's that smell?

STEWART: Rotting meat.

URSULA: What is it, Stew?

STEWART: An inscription. It's in Arabic.

URSULA: What does it say, Malek?

MALEK: It says: 'Do not say we were killed for nothing. What do we live for if not the words that are spoken of us when we die. We live for what is written by our deeds.'

GEORDIE steps back and snaps something with his foot.

URSULA: What was that?

GEORDIE: Sticks. The floor's covered in them.

STEWART: It's not sticks, Geordie.

GEORDIE: Bones.

URSULA: The hand of the lord was on me, and laid me down in a valley of bones.

GEORDIE: The Generals?

STEWART scans room with torch.

STEWART: These are more recent. There's a check shirt.

URSULA: They're human bones? What's that?

STEWART: ID card.

He passes it to MALEK.

Don't think the ancient Greeks carried ID cards.

MALEK: Salaam Mohammed. Born 17 July, 1958.

URSULA: This place was a no-go area under Saddam. No wonder.

A shadow falls across them. They become aware of the offstage presence.

STEWART: Sheikh Kuffa?

MALEK: He says the British might be the biggest tribe in Basra, but here, he is boss. Put down your guns.

STEWART: Won't he step into the temple?

MALEK: Perhaps he would like to preserve his distance, and his options. You British have not exactly earned his trust.

STEWART and GEORDIE put their guns down.

STEWART: Tell him we did not wish to show any disrespect.

MALEK: (*Translating STEWART literally.*) Lem yaksidoo ay qilet ihtiram.

STEWART: We come not as soldiers, Sheikh Kuffa, but to pay a debt.

MALEK: Lem naati hunaa ke-djinood, Shekh el-Kuffa, j'inaa le-dafih el-hisaab…

STEWART: A debt we have incurred by our own rashness and fear.

MALEK: Hisab el ladi kadaynah min waraa wadiyatana wa khawfuna.

STEWART: We have brought the blood money.

MALEK: Lakaad jalabnaa filoos el-dem.

STEWART: And in return we ask for the safe release of Sayed's wife and son.

MALEK: Wa fi al-mukaabil nureed itlaq sarāh zawjet saaed wa waladihe.

STEWART: Before I give you the money, I must know that they are with you and alive.

The drone of approaching airplanes.

What are they Geordie?

GEORDIE: Sound like F18 Hornets, boss. Americans.

STEWART: Must be on the flight path to Bagdhad.

MALEK: The woman and child are with them, he says. They are in the boot of his car.

URSULA: In this heat? Jesus, get them out of there –

URSULA rushes out.

STEWART: Geordie, go with her, I'll wait here with the Sheikh.

Exit GEORDIE. STEWART and MALEK stand facing each other. The drone of the airplanes grows louder.

A breathless GEORDIE re-enters the temple.

GEORDIE: Boss, it's a blue on blue, get out. This is the target. The temple. All of you.

Pause. The shadow of the Sheikh begins to fade.

STEWART: No, Geordie, you leave.

GEORDIE: But you'll all die.

STEWART: Go!

GEORDIE: Malek?

MALEK: If it be written by the hand of God –

STEWART: Go Geordie.

MALEK: – then might all our unhappiness die with us too.

STEWART: Go! Get out!

Pause.

GEORDIE: No, boss, I'm staying with you.

11: THE EDITOR'S OFFICE

Pause.

URSULA: I thought a documentary. The Sunday night slot.

TARIQ: There is certainly some interesting stuff in there, Ursula.

URSULA: The true story of Alpha Unit. Stewart's, I mean Sergeant McDonald's story as the main story. He made the decisions. The most interesting character.

TARIQ: And I can see why this media relations major is so keen to get his hands on the recordings.

URSULA: You're not going to let them have them?

TARIQ: What was it he said, Sophie? He wants to 'preserve the men's reputations as heroes'.

URSULA: He wants to preserve his backside after the bullshit story the army put out.

TARIQ: He threatened you with the Official Secrets Act, didn't he Sophie?

URSULA: They gave their consent. You're not going to let him have them, are you Tariq?

TARIQ: Of course not. The recordings are your property.

URSULA: Glad to see you still believe in the freedom of the press.

TARIQ: I solemnly believe that the freedom of the press is the cornerstone of democracy. My commitment is to our listenership. They have a right to know the truth –

URSULA: And you said three dead Brits and I could have top slot. I've got four.

TARIQ: And that commitment entails maintaining the highest levels of integrity.

URSULA: Of course.

Pause.

Of course, Tariq. (*Beat.*) What are you saying?

TARIQ: I'm sorry, Sophie, I think I shall take that coffee after all.

Beat.

SOPHIE: But your heart, Tariq?

TARIQ: To hell with my heart: double espresso. Tell them to make it strong. These Italians never make it strong enough.

URSULA: What's wrong, Tariq?

Exit SOPHIE.

TARIQ: You seem to have got very close to McDonald?

URSULA: It was natural, given the circumstances. I got close to them all –

TARIQ: But him in particular.

URSULA fights the impulse to respond.

So, it could be seen to compromise your objectivity.

URSULA: What?

TARIQ: In some quarters. If we are to put out material that contradicts the official version, we must be seen to be whiter than white.

URSULA: What are you saying?

TARIQ: All I'm saying, Ursula, is that your closeness to
McDonald could raise questions, in certain quarters, about
the objectivity of the piece. Much of it relies on your word.

TARIQ picks up SOPHIE's log.

The actual recordings could back up either version.

URSULA: Is that why you wanted that log? So you could re-cut
it to suit their story?

TARIQ: No, as I said, I wanted to see what we had and when
and where each recording was made.

URSULA: Jesus Tariq, who's to know how close me and Stew
were? He's dead.

TARIQ: So, you'd be willing to sacrifice that little truth in the
service of the greater truth?

URSULA: Of course, because that stuff's not important.

TARIQ: Well what about the greater truth in all of this?

URSULA: What greater truth? This is the greater truth.

TARIQ picks up an official report.

TARIQ: The MoD issued a statement saying how these four
servicemen died, under friendly fire, escorting three
Bedouin through the British zone in order to deliver blood
money to save a Bedouin's family.

URSULA: They shot three unarmed Bedouin dead.

TARIQ: The soldiers died heroes.

URSULA: They were heroes, but –

TARIQ: One when the car went over a mine –

URSULA: An unexploded American shell –

TARIQ: One presumed lost in a sandstorm –

URSULA: After attempting to rape a journalist.

TARIQ: And the remaining two at the rendezvous which had been inadvertently arranged at an archaeological site Saddam had been using as a weapons dump.

URSULA: Weapons dump? There were no weapons. It was a two-and-a-half-thousand-year old body dump. And the Allies have just dumped more bodies on it.

TARIQ: Their story is largely true.

URSULA: Apart from the bits that are blatant lies. Christ, isn't it our job to report the truth?

TARIQ: But is the truth so simple –

URSULA: No, it's complicated, but just because it is complex, does not mean we should avoid it.

TARIQ: Your version tarnishes the reputations of four military heroes.

URSULA: They were heroic, but in a much more human way. The public are not idiots. They understand moral complexity.

TARIQ: The discrepancies you wish to expose strip the men of the dignity the official version affords them. And the Government would be only too happy to seize upon your contradicting of the official version of events to sidetrack us and the public from the real issues –

URSULA: Which are?

TARIQ: Why we are there in the first place. That's the greater truth. They lied to us.

URSULA: Is that a fact or your personal opinion?

TARIQ: Fact.

URSULA: Then how come you can't make it stick?

TARIQ: We will.

URSULA: The public has a right to know all the stories.

TARIQ: This is more important than the public. It's between us and them. It's about the freedom of the press.

Pause.

URSULA: So, you're going to hand the recordings over?

TARIQ: Of course I'm not. But I think you should consider it.

URSULA: That would be a betrayal of those men.

TARIQ: Sadly, they're dead.

URSULA: I thought I could rely on you, Tariq.

TARIQ: You can Ursula. It's your best interests I have at heart. (*Beat.*) There's talk upstairs of your next posting. (*Pause.*) Some felt your reports from Iraq were less than value for money.

URSULA: Is that a threat?

TARIQ: That is friendly advice.

URSULA: I don't believe this –

TARIQ: I defended you, Ursula, I think you are an excellent and assiduous –

URSULA: Thank you. I must be going –

TARIQ: They suggested Brussels –

URSULA: I've got a train to catch –

TARIQ: Ursula –

URSULA: I've got to meet someone –

URSULA gets up and rapidly gathers her things.

12: THE HOME

A kitchen. Enter JEANNIE followed by URSULA.

URSULA: Sorry I'm late. Held up in London.

JEANNIE: This way, Miss Gunn.

URSULA: Ursula, call me Ursula, Mrs McDonald, please. And I wanted to come.

JEANNIE: Jeannie.

URSULA: Jeannie.

They shake hands. Pause.

JEANNIE: Tea?

URSULA: Thanks.

JEANNIE goes to make tea.

JEANNIE: You're not like the rest of them.

URSULA: Who?

JEANNIE puts biscuits on a plate.

JEANNIE: The other ones.

URSULA: Journalists?

JEANNIE goes to fridge, fetches milk and pours it into a jug.

Have there been others?

JEANNIE: At first. Then they lost interest. Nothing to dig up. Someone died trying to do someone a favour. Not enough dirt, I expect. Then the next tragedy happened and they were off.

JEANNIE pours boiling water into teapot.

You were with Stewart?

URSULA: Yes.

JEANNIE: In Iraq?

URSULA: Yes.

JEANNIE: Milk? Sugar?

URSULA: Thanks.

JEANNIE: You're from Ireland?

URSULA: Northern.

JEANNIE: Stewart served there.

URSULA: I know. He told me.

JEANNIE: I mean, we lived there. (*Beat.*) Funny, he didn't usually talk about it. I think things happen in the army. Between men. They don't like to talk to outsiders about it.

URSULA: Yes.

JEANNIE: I expect he began to treat you as one of the boys. I don't know why he went back out. He's seen so little of Tom and Ella growing up. (*Beat.*) He said it was the overstretch. Undermanned. Under-resourced. If he's talked to you, I don't know why you want to talk to me. I'm not very interesting. Or is this what you wanted? Some tears? He didn't have to go. I knew that. I let him believe that I believed he had to, but I knew he didn't. No one should have had to go out there. But it was easier for that to be the reason. Easier to go for the wrong reasons than confront the real ones. And now he's dead and a hero for fifteen minutes and I'll have to keep all this stuff inside me. The children miss him. But then he's barely been here all their lives. We've coped with that, we'll cope with this. I've got to pick them up from football in twenty minutes and look at the state of me. Is this what you wanted? Is this what you wanted?

URSULA: I came here because I wanted you to know that your husband was a good man –

JEANNIE: I know that. I know that. How dare you! I don't need a journalist to tell me.

URSULA: Yes. I'm sorry. (*Beat.*) He saved my life three times. The third time, at Kabro a Generals, I think he knew something was going to happen. Like Malek's daughter and her white dress –

JEANNIE: I beg your pardon?

URSULA: He sent me and Geordie out of the temple. Geordie ran back. He wasn't meant to. Stewart wanted to save people. He saved that mother and child.

JEANNIE: Men who want to save people are dangerous to be around.

URSULA: I came here because – because perhaps you haven't been told all the details surrounding the death of your husband. I went to Geordie's mother. I had a tape of him reading a letter he had written to her. The letter was never passed on to her. I think because in it he admitted killing a Bedouin at a checkpoint. I felt she should know the truth, but also that she should hear him tell her he loved her which he hadn't done since he'd left home.

JEANNIE: You have a great commitment to the truth.

URSULA: Stewart gave me this before he died.

URSULA passes her STEWART's tobacco tin.

He kept everything that was important to him in it.

JEANNIE: A candle stub, tablets, more tablets –

URSULA: Aspirin.

JEANNIE: An Absolut Vodka miniature. Empty.

URSULA: Helped Dangermouse as best it could –

JEANNIE: Some other bits.

URSULA: There's a photo.

JEANNIE: Yes. Thank you. I see.

URSULA: You and the kids.

JEANNIE: He always used to keep a condom in it. I've looked in his tobacco tin before. I know what he kept there. I know that isn't the picture. Perhaps you should keep the tin?

URSULA: I don't smoke.

JEANNIE: Well, perhaps Tom would like it. Please, I have to pick my children up. I must get ready.

URSULA: Of course, I'm sorry, I should be going.

URSULA gathers her things.

Jeannie?

JEANNIE: Yes.

URSULA: He loved you.

JEANNIE: He told you?

URSULA: Yes.

JEANNIE: When?

Beat.

URSULA: The morning, the morning he died.

Beat.

JEANNIE: Thank you for saying that, Ursula. Even if it's not true. Perhaps, if you're allowed, if you had a recording of him. His voice.

URSULA: I brought one. I made it for you.

JEANNIE: Thank you.

Beat.

URSULA: Goodbye.

JEANNIE: Goodbye.

Exit URSULA. JEANNIE goes to CD player. She loads CD. STEWART appears.

STEWART: It had been a day of miracles, the bull headed creature, a djinn or even an ancient god of Babylon – Marduk or Baal or the God of a Thousand Faces, Malek said – who made the desert flow with water. And then Malek's return, and then the Ma'adan who had so little, whose very world had dried up under Saddam, yet for us they had rolled out the carpet and celebrated our deliverance with olives and kofta balls and water from their deepest secret wells, water that tasted like the finest wines. And afterwards, we lay on the floor of the desert looking up at the heavens. No mediation. Nothing in between us and eternity. At peace.

THE END